Communication Skills For

Workplace Trainers

The New Trainer's Textbook

Ken Owens

Testimonials

"We all become complacent at some point in what we do. As a speaker, you need to review yourself and your presentation on a regular basis. This book is packed full of tips and ideas which will certainly *up* your game. Gone are the days of the rah-rah motivational speaker; they are a dime a dozen on YouTube. Speakers these days need to be educating. Companies want you to help their employees, share lessons and knowledge that you have acquired over the years, and then show them how to apply those skills into their work and personal life. This book is a great tool for you to review your material, and add value, so that you deliver when you speak."

Alam Ghafoor, **United Kingdom**
Trainer, International Business Consultant, Author

"I found the book detailed and helpful, yet thorough and easy-to-understand. It covers many key areas of speaking and teaching so that even a beginner can become a confident and effective trainer. I wish I had read this book before some of my classroom sessions. The key points that are enumerated and the reminders presented as checklists are very helpful for even the most experienced trainer."

Bill Perry, USA, Retired, University Donor Relations

"This book is an informative and refreshing approach, providing skills for trainers who wish to inspire as well as inform."

Rhonda Carlson, **USA,** Performance Coach, Author, Educator

Education / Professional Development / Training

Communication Skills For Workplace Trainers

The New Trainer's Textbook

© 2023 by Ken Owens

Las Vegas, NV   USA
www.TheKenOwens.com

Cover Design by: Olayemi Bolaji
Ken's Headshot by: Chuck Rounds

Personal Dynamics Publishing
www.PersonalDynamicsPublishing.com

ISBN: 979-8-9888867-0-9

Author's Note: *This book is not intended to provide medical or mental health advice, diagnosis, or treatment.*

Dedication

This book is dedicated to my nieces Nicole and Ryann. Always stand up and speak your mind!

Also, to all those new trainers who have to deliver content as part of their job. This book will give you a solid foundation and remove your fears, while making it a rewarding addition to your resume. Most importantly, insuring those who hear you have a fun and educational experience.

Table of Contents

Preface

This textbook will help those who need to speak effectively as a trainer and educator in the workplace. It deals not so much with *What to Say* as *How to Say It.* It is geared to prepare those newly hired workplace trainers who wish to expand their speaking and training skills in: Sales, Human Resources, Clergy, Nonprofit, Government, and Small Business.

Some say training is an art. I say it is more a blend between art and science. There is a definite degree of mechanics, psychology, and physiology that has to go into the foundation and delivery of a properly executed training presentation. To me, it is the correct blending of all those elements which then, makes the finished program look and sound like a masterful piece of art. Although, like honing your craft as an artist or athlete; there is much practice which needs to be put forth behind the fundamentals, principles, and ideas shared within this book.

None of the concepts in this book can be accomplished without the proper mental conditioning of you, the trainer. You need to dispel, right now, any notions of fear and think of the public speaking component of training, as a relaxed friendly chat with your friends. It's mind-blowing that public speaking is still the number one fear of people today. Speaking is a vital component to many careers, and the better equipped you are in this area, the higher your income and greater earning potential.

If this book stimulates you to work toward becoming a more effective trainer, or to make that task easier and more fun, and to dispel any erroneous notions often associated with speaking and training; then my objectives for this book will be fulfilled. The purpose of this book is to portray the principles of designing and delivering a training program for the person who is eager to be an effective workplace trainer. One must thoroughly understand and apply the principles of content, audience, and speaking contained within these pages in order to reach your objective. Whether you plan to train an audience of 1 or 5,000; this book is for you!

~ *Ken*

"Let no one be discouraged by the belief there is nothing one man or one woman can do against the enormous array of the world's ills: against misery and ignorance, injustice, and violence. Few will have the greatness to bend history itself; but each of us can work to change small portions of events, and in the total of these acts will be written the history of this generation.

It is from numberless diverse acts of courage and belief that human history is shaped. Each time a person stands up for an idea, or acts to improve the lots of others, or strikes out against injustice, that person sends a tiny ripple of hope, and crossing each other form a million different centers of energy and daring. Those ripples build a current which can sweep down the mightiest walls of oppression and resistance."

Robert F. Kennedy

Chapter 1

Workplace Trainer vs. Speaker

> *"I hear and I forget. I see and I remember. I do and I understand."* ~ Confucius

Perception

You work at a fairly large corporation and your boss tells you one of the following two scenarios:

1.   "Tuesday morning is a mandatory meeting in the conference room from 9am until 11am. We have a speaker coming to address the team." Or,

2.   "Tuesday morning is a mandatory meeting in the conference room from 9am until 11am. We have a trainer coming to address the team."

What are your thoughts, feelings, assumptions, and expectations when you hear statement #1? What are your thoughts, feelings, assumptions, and expectations when you hear statement #2? Do you have any preconceived notions on the differences between a speaker and a trainer; or are they both the same? What previous encounters have you had in situations with a *speaker* or a *trainer*? Do you think your previous individual experiences might influence your answers to these questions? Which scenario above do you think will have a more powerful positive set of expectations for the team; even far before knowing anything about the person coming to address the team on Tuesday morning?

Author's Opinion

My personal biases are quite strong on this subject. That is why I wanted you to seriously think about those two scenarios before I share my feelings. The point here is for you to realize that you will encounter these biases while delivering your presentations; and you must address these varying opinions within your audience.

When I hear the word *speaker*, I immediately think of a rah-rah motivational style fluff presentation. Like Network Marketing rallies or Sunday morning tele-evangelist pump-you-up mass hypnosis feel-good encounters. All of which I have had previous negative experiences. I have walked out of a three-day *Big Name Speaker's* weekend on the first morning because of the 'I'm OK, you're OK,' 'rub the shoulders of the person next to you' garbage. During the 1970's to early 2000's, corporations spent tens of millions of dollars hiring speakers to come in and make their employees feel good, in an effort to motivate the staff for higher productivity. That was when companies had money to throw away on ineffective programs like those, which really only brought short term effects. Most of that rah-rah feel-good motivation leaves the person when they walk out the door from the event. True and lasting change comes when an employee is motivated from within.

When I hear the word *trainer* or *workplace trainer*, I immediately think of teacher, educator, or professor. I assume I am going to learn something. I come prepared with a pen and notepad because I expect to take useful notes which I can implement into my daily activities. In statement #2, my mindset walking into the conference room on Tuesday morning would be the same as if I was walking into a college classroom – open minded with the excitement of leaning new concepts.

Now that you have heard my biases, do you agree or disagree with me? Do you see how labels can induce a sub-conscious expectation; both positive and negative? Those audience expectations will be the filter through which they judge your presentation. Your job as a compelling speaker or trainer is to overcome those negative expectations, while harnessing those positive expectations within your audience. That is what will elevate you to a professional communicator. That is what you will learn in this book!

Speaker is Everywhere

Even with the discussion we just had, part of the ingrained problem is that the word *speaker* is used universally in workplace America. There are speaker's bureaus, not trainer's bureaus, and the word is used interchangeably within the industry by meeting planners and booking agents. So, how do you make sure you are not left out of any booking or employment opportunities? Here is what I do:

1.   I have **Author/Speaker/Trainer** listed on my business cards. I cover all the bases!

2.   When a meeting planner calls to hire me for an event, I ask their expectations. Are they looking for motivation or education? If they only want rah-rah, I

decline the event. I tell the agent/planner, "When your client is looking for their staff to learn key growth concepts and actionable take-away items, then call me back and hire me at that time."

What do you think happens in the mind of the meeting planner when I tell them the above statement? They are shocked! Most speakers prostitute themselves out for every dollar at any gig. When I give the response above, I set myself apart from the rest of the herd. It gives me an image of exclusivity. And guess what, when the planner calls back to book me, after discussing my comments with their client, I can ask for a higher fee!

If your goal is to become a high-energy motivational speaker, then that is OK too. In today's economy, corporations might be looking for a more definite return on their training dollars, thus probably education over motivation. It will take you a longer period of time to reach the motivational notoriety level of a Les Brown, than it would to be recognized as an effective workplace trainer.

> ## My prices are based on my talent, not on your budget!

Is There a Difference?

Is there really a difference between the labels speaker, teacher, and trainer to substantiate a bias? Research seems to say a definite yes! Bill Gove who was known as *the father of professional speaking* said this:

"Other speakers are not my heroes. Most of them think they're teachers. I watch stand-up comics. These people know they're in show business."

This quote insinuates, from one of the top speakers who trained other speakers for decades, that speaking is more entertainment and show business, rather than sharing substantive information. Looking at many motivational speakers today, it seems the more charismatic they are, the bigger they get, which really has no correlation to the information they impart.

In an article titled, *The Difference Between Speaking and Teaching*, Derek Featherstone shares that speaking is telling and showing the audience examples of things you have done. And he says with teaching, you create an experience for the audience, while thinking more about their previous knowledge and caring about their understanding of the subject. Derek said:

"If speaking is about the speaker having and giving knowledge to the audience, then teaching is about them [the audience] and you crafting an educational experience that helps them discover new things, and that helps them create new knowledge for themselves from within."

So where does training fall in this labeling debate? Maybe training is a hybrid of the other two? Maybe training is the best of both? If speaking is about sharing ideas and experiences in a story format to motivate your audience; and teaching is more goal-focused with an assessment component to rate audience comprehension; then truly workplace training is the culmination of both. Tai Goodwin said in an article, *"Brilliant teachers have a deep understanding of their learners, solid practical experience and a growing knowledge of their topic."* All which are qualities of a brilliant workplace trainer too!

There is nothing wrong with any of these three labels, because each are an opportunity to help your audience learn. Each has its own context, and that context will be determined by how you present the materials. Your level of subject matter expertise, your understanding of the baseline knowledge of each audience participant, your ability to weave interactive practical applications into your training session; coupled with your ability to assess at a testing level, how your participants have grasped your concepts, will determine your success as an effective workplace trainer. Training is about changing behaviors, and behavior changes require more tools and effort than a few slides and bragging how a speaker did it. Training is about how your audience members can do it. When training has been done well, your participants will have a heightened sense of inner confidence, because they learned a new skill or concept.

Verbiage in This Book

The word *speaker* and *trainer* will be used interchangeably in this book. However, the goal is to focus on your job as a workplace trainer using the act of speaking as a method to present your program.

Section I: *Speaking Fundamentals*

Chapter 2

Speaking Characteristics

Public Speaking Defined

What is public speaking? It is speaking to a collection of individuals. Its purposes are to convey thought, to mold opinion, to awaken feeling, or to sell a product or service. Any one or all of these purposes may be present in any given presentation, but in all cases there are thought patterns to be conveyed to your listener. Those thought patterns may be in the form of *exposition* (detailed information – educational, workplace training), *argument* (stirring strong emotions in the listener), or *appeal* (asking for listeners to do something – buy your product, donate to your nonprofit, join an organization). Public speaking as it pertains to the component of workplace training, is *speaking in public with the purpose of educating and persuading*.

Test of the Best Public Speaking

You might be speaking to ten, one hundred, or one thousand people in your audience. How best do you speak to them for the purposes of instructing, convincing, or persuading? This question is best answered by asking, "How best do you speak to them as an individual?" Therefore, the criteria for the best group public speaking are those criteria which make for the best individual conversation, not the showiest or entertainingly dramatic (unless rah-rah motivation), but best from the standpoint of individual effectiveness and comprehension. In the act of conveying thought to your listener, what constitutes effectiveness in individual conversation? Among other things, a good conversationalist must possess the qualities of clearness, directness, simplicity, vivacity, spontaneity, and sincerity. Hence, these are the same qualities needed for speaking in training scenarios.

What Public Speaking is Not?

We are going to dispel any rumors of flamboyant or systematic behaviors making a good speaker. A pleasing and caring voice is needed, but one does not need to have a musical voice; that is a good thing, because you don't want to hear me singing in the shower. Grace is desirable, but you don't need to be a model; pretty gestures do not carry a cause or win a verdict. Nor is there any ready-made prescription to become an instant speaker.

Many beginning speakers seek courses and books in the hope of finding some type of patented pattern or pre-packaged system which they can clone to make them a proficient speaker. Let any thought of a quick fix, method, or system be removed from your mind right now! Only your own method, the expression of your individuality, will make you a powerful and effective speaker. Run the other direction from any teacher or program which offers you a 'speaker in a box' program; you will become nothing more than a parrot or machine, and you will lose any sense of credibility and sincerity from your audience. Be yourself, not a mere imitator. Aim for the best and most effective expression of *yourself* within the context of each of your presentations.

As you will learn throughout the chapters of this book, certain principles are fundamental, but expression will be as varied as individualities. Your individuality is the *art* component of speaking, while the fundamental principles are the *science* of speaking. Those two components, blended together along with much practice, will produce a successful speaker.

Above all, within the context of public speaking, remove any ambition to become eloquent. Who cares if your words are so flowery that people say you, "soar among the unicorns and drizzle the floor with glitter!" Seeking eloquence in speaking tends to bring personal ego, phoniness, and careless admiration, like a Sunday morning televangelist. Your goal, within the context of this book, and our goal in workplace training, is to convince, inform, and persuade your listeners; not to be an eloquent entertainer.

The Basis of Public Speaking

Public speaking, thus, being the communication of thought, therefore assumes you have something to say (Section III will address content creation). Your message must be presented to the listener's mind in a clear and vivid manner, and at the particular time which it needs to be conveyed to your audience. Public speaking then can be referred to as the art and science of thinking aloud. If there is one thing which all audiences hate, no matter whether it is a co-worker in a meeting, or a trainer on a stage; it's the chronic talker who has nothing to say and is forever saying it. We all know those people who just talk for the purpose of hearing themselves talk! It is in the preparation of clear, orderly, and intense thinking patterns which will hold the attention of your listeners.

> **"Blessed are they who have nothing to say, and who cannot be persuaded to say it."** ~ James Russell Lowell

Speaking effectively is a very complicated and exacting procedure which requires specific training and makes definite demands on the speaker's thought, voice, and action. No other human activity requires as high a degree of concentration and coordination as does the art and science of public speaking. Throughout the entire speaking process, each of the components which we will be discussing in this book will need to function as a single unit. You, the trainer, while speaking, have specific bioorganic and neuromuscular functions which need to operate at their optimum performance in order to deliver an effective presentation. For example, if you wake up with a temporary bio-organic disorder (such as a head cold), then your voice and speech delivery will not be able to effectively communicate your thought message. As the speaker, you may have habitual defects such as: stuttering, slurred speech, a raspy smokers-voice; or other issues which will not allow for a clear flow of your thoughts to your listening audience. In any speaking situation, it is voice and action which are the modes through which thought reaches its objective. Your thoughts are your message, which you put forth to reach your listeners.

A speech situation is one in which someone is speaking, and one or more people are mentally reacting to what the speaker is saying. Therefore, a speech situation does not exist when someone stands before a group and talks while those in the audience look in their general direction but are not being stimulated by what the speaker is saying. Effective speaking requires mental action on the part of both the speaker and the listener. A speaker does not literally transfer their thoughts or ideas to the mind of a listener. A listener must be stimulated to react mentally to what a speaker is saying. Speech is a *stimulating*, not a *transferring* process. The specific purpose of a speaker while conducting a workplace training program, is to cause the listener to arrive, through the process of active reasoning, at certain conclusions which will stimulate them to react in accordance with the specific purpose of the presentation.

In many speaking scenarios, a speaker has been accredited with a successful effort to speak well, but attributed the failure of the audience to actively respond to the stupidity of the listeners (we will address this more in an upcoming chapter). However, an intelligent and effective trainer recognizes they are the pacemaker, which upon them rests the responsibility of stimulating to action, those who are in the audience. In the preparation and presentation of a training program, an effective trainer must clearly differentiate between the responsibilities of them and the listeners.

What beginning speakers and trainers fail to remember is that there is a universally recognized Law of Motor Response which states, "For every stimulus there is a definite reaction, the nature of which depends upon two factors: first, the nature of the stimulus; second, the past experiences of the reacting person." You as the trainer have complete control over the first of these, and through careful research and preparation of your audience, you will learn how to conquer the second point as well. There is really only one factor by which the effectiveness of your presentation can be determined, that is the reaction which it produces in those who listen to it – both short term and long term. Keeping in mind that your desired result will be different based on the type of presentation you are giving – educational vs. persuasion.

It is the underlying attitude of this book, to follow the advice from Ancient Greek teachers of speech:

> **"Stand up in order that you may be seen.**
> **Speak up in order that you may be heard.**
> **Shut up in order that you may be appreciated!"**

As necessary as speaking is in many professions, there is entirely too much of it, and too many people ramble on endlessly. Remember this rule, ***the need is quantitatively less and qualitatively better***.

Throughout this book, much emphasis will be placed upon definite objectives. Often speakers fail because they do not have a specific objective in mind during the planning and presentation process of their speech; however, you as a workplace trainer will not have those issues because Section III of this book will help you design a solid program. One should know exactly what they wish to say, and they should also know how to say it in order to secure the desired reaction from the audience. Effective speaking is still a fine art. Like all of the arts, it rests upon a foundation of scientific principles.

Contrary to popular opinion, good trainers are made, not born; and effective speaking comes as a direct result of thoughtful planning and persistent practice!

What are the traits which characterize effective speaking in workplace training? How can we analyze and differentiate traits between effective and ineffective speaking? How can one speaker, given a subject, inform, delight, and exhilarate an audience, while another speaker, given the same subject, bore an audience to death? Once we have determined the necessary components to become effective, how will you, as a student of the training profession, measure up to the concept that we have formed? By the end of this book, you will be aware of all the traits and tools which you will need to become a powerful speaker and dynamic workplace trainer; you will then need to add your subject matter and lots of practice.

What are the specific characteristics and personality traits which develop into effective speaking?

1.   First of all, they are a person who is wide awake mentally, emotionally, and physically. They believe that what they are saying is worthy of the listener's most concentrated attention. Their number one concern is to think, emote, and move in such a manner as to cause the audience to react to the ideas presented, based on the planned desired outcome.

2.   They are thoroughly informed on the subject. They have to be a subject matter expert! They are a diligent reader, a keen observer, and have a wide variety of interests and experiences. They know how to relate their

experiences to the subject matter; thus, making for a very personal presentation.

3.   They are deeply interested in their subject. They exhibit this interest by becoming enthused when they speak.

4.   They are a clear speaker. They know what they want to say, and they say it in a simple, straight-forward manner. Because they are clear in their own thinking, they never confuse the listener with inconsistent statements, irrelevant materials, long and involved sentences, or through the misuse of words.

5.   They possess a strong imagination. It is easy for them to visualize realities which cannot be shown under the current circumstances; thus, they are able to paint word-pictures which stimulate the listeners to form appropriate concepts.

6.   They have a good speaking voice. It is agreeably pitched, adequately strong, and rich in quality. They articulate clearly and distinctly. They pace the rate to the needs of the material being discussed; following the psychological principle of that which is most important requires a slower rate of speech. They know how to secure favorable attention from the audience through the use of their voice.

7.   They have control over their body. They know how to use their body as a mechanism through which to further express ideas more effectively. They use body movements and non-verbal communication for the purpose of emphasizing the ideas expressed in words. Their

thoughts and movements are highly coordinated and work together as one.

8.   They select their words carefully. Words are chosen based on their meaning and sound. They are aware of the psychological effects which certain words and sounds can have on an audience.

9.   They are well poised. Their mental and physical posture indicates that they believe they are capable of saying what they want to say. They are at ease as they stand before the audience, and they move about the stage at ease. Because an effective trainer is confident in themselves, they foster that same confidence on the part of the audience. They are very sure of themselves, but are not over aggressive or egotistical! They speak confidently and directly to each listener.

10.   They are courteous and sincere. They treat each listener as if that person were their personal guest. They stimulate the interest of the listeners in a way which causes them to want to come back for more.

11.   They are original. They devise ways of enabling the audience to give undivided attention to what they are saying through the use of illustrations, comparisons, colorful descriptions, and funny incidents.

12.   They emphasize their main points so that they may be easily remembered. They are versed in the application of the Forms of Emphasis and use them in appropriate situations.

Will Power

Now that we have defined the twelve fundamental characteristics of effective speaking, how do you acquire them? Proficiency in effective communication, as in any other field of study, comes as a result of proper training plus the application of persistent effort. Will power is always a prerequisite to the success in any field. Will power is not a substitute for ability and training; it is just as integral in the success equation:

Success in ANY field = Training + Ability + Will Power

Without willpower, even the most talented and well trained speaker will never rise above the level of mediocrity. An effective trainer must, after much preparation has been put into the development of the presentation materials, train their conscious and subconscious mind to function at peak performance. They must prepare their body to serve as a medium to further express their ideas, while always exerting themselves to their utmost potential, or they will fall short of their greatest possibilities. Thoroughness in preparation, an interesting subject (or making a dull subject interesting), and adequate training in delivery are not the only determining factors for an effective training program. In addition to these indispensable factors, the trainer must WILL themselves to do their best on every single occasion.

Rising to the top in any field is only possible when there is a personally motivated *will* to continuously improve. If you are a student in a classroom situation using this as a textbook, it is my heartfelt hope that your professor is one to motivate and encourage you to pursue speaking and training, while instilling a desire for life-long improvement. If you are reading this book on your own for personal and professional development purposes; you have to look deep within yourself to find the reason you are drawn to the art and science of speaking and training. Use that reason as your inner voice, your personal cheerleader, to harness your power of will to achieve success in the field of workplace training.

Learning to speak is just like exercise, you have to push yourself to reach new goals on an ongoing basis. It has been shown that a person practicing a topic or exercising at an ordinary rate will not reach their maximum ability. The higher the skill, the higher the bar for practice and determination must be. Daily practice in any field will not ensure improvement; that daily practice must have a goal to do 'one better' than the day before. That is how you release weight or gain muscle mass when exercising. The same holds true with any form of mental conditioning and mastering any task, like effective speaking. Remember, each new step that you take seems to cost more than the previous step; but with each step, you are rising closer and closer to the achievement of your particular goal.

Research studies have shown that intense effort, properly applied to the details of the task at hand was a necessary condition for improvement in learning as it pertained to typing on a computer keyboard or piano playing skills. Only when students are in optimum condition (physically and mentally), feeling good and applying their best efforts to that task at hand, did they succeed in inventing new and better methods of hand/finger control or varying their former methods in a new and helpful way. The plateaus in the learning curve, or periods of non-improvement encountered in the learning, were brought about by a combination of causes, primarily among them was found to be a decrease in the amount of effort applied to the details of the work. This prevented the students from achieving higher levels of proficiency and brought about careless mistakes.

Students in any field can overcome these negative plateaus in a learning curve if they maintain an elevated level of interest in the subject and have the proper encouragement and motivation to succeed. A student's inner drive for improvement was found to be just as important as external encouragement. One profits by continuous practice in any field only in the proportion as we arouse our will and intention to do so. As we know from physical exercise examples, the mere repetition of an act, even on a daily basis, is by no means sufficient to bring about an improvement in the development and mastering of any act. Repetition (practice), plus the willpower to grow to a higher level (achieve new heights of success), is what it takes to become an expert in any field.

These general learning psychology references apply to any field and are of particular importance to the scientific fundament foundations for public speaking. Skill in speaking is acquired. It depends upon a keen skill of thinking and mastering techniques of expression through the scientific mechanics of voice and action.

The little rant here on the importance of will; should not be taken in any way to negate the importance of content, voice training, skill in non-verbal communication, or thorough preparation of subject, and audience comprehension; but as stated before, these factors once carefully developed, are still inadequate unless coupled with your inner urge to continuously improve. Above all remember, willingness is not a substitute for any of the essential elements required in the preparation phase, but it is the final factor which, more than anything else, determines the effectiveness of any training presentation. It will become your goal as an effective professional workplace trainer to improve each time you appear before an audience.

> "I have made it an established rule to do my best on every occasion and in every company: To impart whatever I know in the most forcible language I could put in it; and by constant practice, and never suffering a careless expression to escape me or attempting to deliver my thoughts without arranging them in the clearest manner, it has become habitual to me." ~ Samuel Johnson

Upcoming Chapters

The upcoming chapters of this book will explore in detail each of the essential elements and the scientific fundamentals which you need to become an effective and powerful workplace trainer. The speaking component of workplace training is an important overall business skill and thus why it is the first section we will master. It's even more important than content creation. It is my desire to properly equip you with the necessary foundational skills. Then in due time, the effective speaking component of workplace training will become habitual for you. By the end of this book, all you will need to do is add your own subject matter and dynamic personality to start educating and persuading audiences all over the world!

Chapter 3

Mind Dynamics

> *"Be careful of your thoughts; they may become words at any moment."* ~ Ira Gassen

The Mechanics of the Mind

The first and most essential element in effective speaking is that of thought. Let's look at the science behind where those thoughts originate. We all know that there is a physical apparatus for thinking – some call it the brain, others call it the mind. Think of the brain as the physical mass which is in our heads; while the mind is the component which resides inside that brain – both our conscious and subconscious. Therefore, thoughts are the output from mind activity inside the brain. It is the power and functioning of this mind machine (brain, mind, thoughts), more than upon any other single factor, where success and/or failure rests for effectiveness in speaking.

We learn from elementary school anatomy and physiology studies that the human body contains a nervous system, the principal component of which is the brain and spinal cord. There are four components of the nervous system which we need to review for their interaction with effective public speaking:

1.   **Cerebrum.** This is the largest and most visible portion of our brain. The cerebrum is comprised of two hemispheres which are connected to each other by a cord of nerve fibers called the corpus callosum. The cerebral cortex is a thin outer layer around the cerebrum where our activities of speech, evaluation of stimuli, conscious thinking, and the control of our muscles occur. Our mental conduct is largely dependent upon what goes on in this region. It is here where most of the conditioning for effectiveness in speech takes place. It is important that this part of the mind machine functions properly so that the speech of an individual will not be impaired.

2.   **Diencephalon.** This is the component of the nervous system which connects the cerebrum (upper brain) to the brain stem (lower brain). Diencephalon has three regions; two of which are important to our study.

A.   The thalamus is considered a relay station for sensory nerve impulses as they travel up the spinal cord on their way to the cerebrum. Some sensations such as pain, pressures, and temperature are evaluated by the thalamus.

B.   The hypothalamus regulates many important body activities. This region controls the autonomic nervous system and regulates emotion, behavior, hunger, thirst, and body temperature.

C.   The third area just to mention is the epithalamus, which contains the pineal gland. The pineal gland is where melatonin is released which helps regulate our biological clock; our sleep-wake cycles.

3.   **Brain Stem.** The brain stem is the lower portion of the brain which connects the diencephalon to the

spinal cord. There are four regions of the brain stem which all provide various connections between the brain and the spinal cord. The reticular activation system (RAS) is found in one of those four regions, called the reticular formation. The RAS is important to our study here because it is responsible for maintaining wakefulness and alertness, and for filtering out unimportant sensory information.

Have you ever experienced the following situation? You are thinking about buying a new car. The minute you put the thought into your mind about buying that particular make, color, and model of car; you suddenly start seeing that same car everywhere you go? That is a function of the RAS – filtering out unimportant information. The unimportant information in this case is every other type of car except the one you are thinking about purchasing.

Dr. Rayma Ditson-Sommer has done extensive research on mind-body connections and how to train the brain for peak performance, including her work with the US Olympic Team. The RAS plays a critical role in this mind-body study of peak performance training. Other responsibilities of the RAS include maintaining muscle tone, regulating visceral motor muscles (visceral organs include heart, bladder and reproductive); plus, the arousal (sexual) and motivational activities in humans. I have had the honor to personally work with Dr. Ditson-Sommer before her death.

4.   **The Limbic System.** The limbic system is a network of neuron fibers which travels through the diencephalon and covers the inside border of the cerebrum. This system imposes an emotional aspect to behaviors, experiences, and memories. Our emotions such as

pleasure, fear, anger, sorrow, and affection are imposed upon events and experiences through the limbic system.

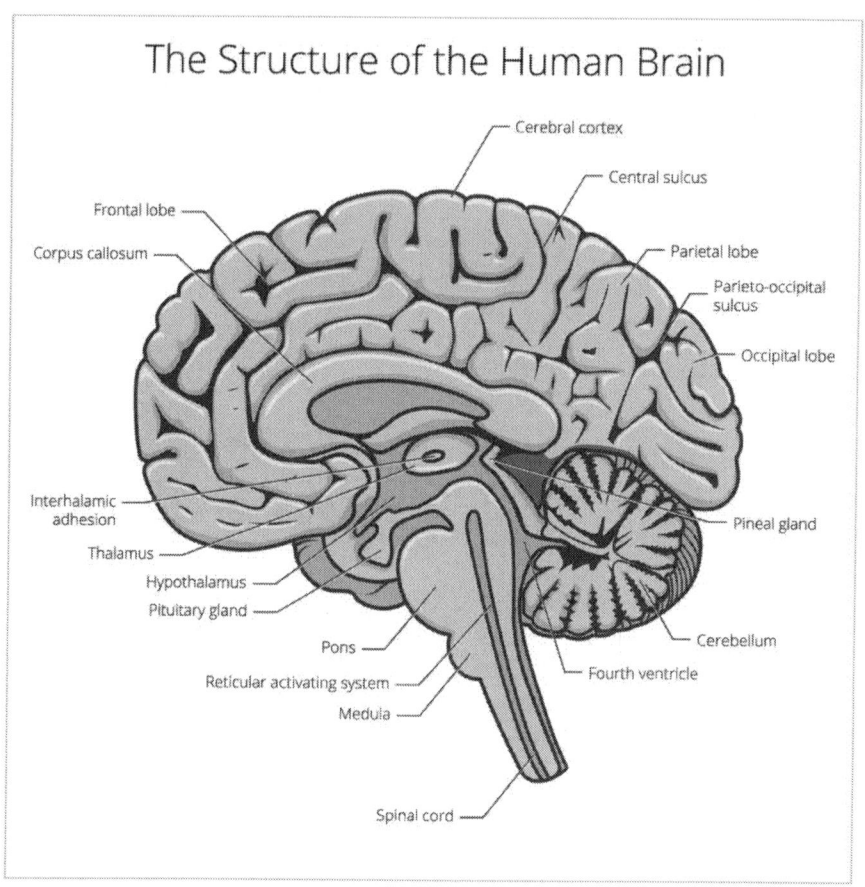

The Structure of the Human Brain

- Cerebral cortex
- Central sulcus
- Frontal lobe
- Corpus callosum
- Parietal lobe
- Parieto-occipital sulcus
- Occipital lobe
- Interhalamic adhesion
- Pineal gland
- Thalamus
- Hypothalamus
- Pituitary gland
- Pons
- Cerebellum
- Reticular activating system
- Fourth ventricle
- Medula
- Spinal cord

The Outcome of Thought

Why do we think? Thought is necessary to develop the means to resolve conflicts. A person thinks in order to cope better with the multitude of situations which present themselves to each of us every day. Thought involves the analysis of perception, ideas, images, concepts, facts, beliefs, imagination, attitudes, purposes, and intentions.

As we have stated, the first requisite for effective speaking is clear thinking. There is no reason for acquiring the skill of speaking and training if there is nothing worthwhile you are going to say. Therefore, your first concern as a trainer should be that of getting and developing an idea, a topic; your subject matter. Your next concern will be the development of a technique for the effective expression of that idea. Those ideas, for which you will create your training programs, might be of your choosing or they may be assigned to you from your employer. Either way, you must attack those ideas with the same vigor and dedication if you are going to be an effective trainer. We have all seen a trainer who is eloquent and entertaining, but when we leave, we have no clue about what they just said. Likewise, we have been to presentations where the subject matter was amazing, but the speaker was so bad we couldn't follow the flow of information. Effective and powerful training is a marriage between idea and delivery.

There are numerous volumes of texts and university based research studies which give detailed explanations on the physiological and psychological aspects as to the how, why, and wherefore of thought processes. This book just wanted to call your attention to a person's mind machine and its main parts, functions, and importance as to how it relates in the effectiveness of successful training.

Language habits are merely thought habits and have their general setting in the bodily integration as a whole. The very nature of thinking involves the use of some set of signs and symbols which differentiate meanings. Even in our most abstract forms of thinking, our dreams, we communicate with symbolic terminology. Many individuals believe that thought and language are inseparable. They hold that belief because it is consistent with their learning and previous experiences. For further insight into the components of thought and language, and how they are different but work cohesively, one should study symbols (symbology) and semantics.

The principal steps of thought in the preparation of a training program are:

1.   Discrimination in evaluating and selecting a subject.

2.   Analyzing the subject into its component parts.

3.   Properly synthesizing the essential elements.

4.   Placing those essential elements into their proper order.

For the sake of emphasis, the first step in effective speaking is a realization of the necessity for clear thinking. The first step in clear thinking is to conceive the desired outcome to be achieved; again, this might be of your choosing or assigned outcomes by your boss. The first step in obtaining that outcome is a thorough analysis and synthesis of all the material to be presented, as well as to what audience.

An effective trainer should bear in mind that although all clear thinkers are not effective speakers, all effective speakers are clear thinkers.

Psychological Factors

There are other essential mind components which must be considered if you are going to perform your task of effective training for the positive satisfaction of your listening audience.

Attention: As previously stated, a speech situation exists only when there is someone speaking, and one or more people are mentally reacting to what is being said. Too often audience members sit and stare at the trainer, but they don't *hear* what is being said. Polite conduct suggests they sit there in a professional manner, but it does not require mental reactions to what the trainer is saying.

A behaviorist contends that the attention of the listener is focused on that to which they are reacting. A trainer is constantly bombarding two of a listener's strongest sensory receivers – those of sight and hearing. The trainer communicates to those two senses through voice and bodily movements. An effective trainer will strive to present their ideas through those two channels of sight and hearing in the most impressive manner in order to best impact those senses of the listener. The trainer's voice must have a pleasant pitch, adequate intensity, rich quality, and sufficient inflection to prevent monotony; all while securing adequate emphasis. In body movement, there must be coordination of gestures which tie in with the thought expressed and adequate facial expressions; all while still being graceful. In all training activities, the speaker is striving to create the desired motor response on the part of the listener. As previously stated, all motor responses are determined by the nature of previous past experiences of the listener. You as a speaker must fully appreciate the nature of the diverse types of stimuli which you present from the standpoint of content and manner of your presentation. You must also do your research ahead of time and know enough about your listening audience to be able to appeal and relate to them through your presentation.

There are two kinds of attention, voluntary and involuntary. The effective trainer gets and holds the involuntary attention of the audience. A listener will not, under normal conditions, and should not be expected to give voluntary attention to a speaker. Voluntary attention yields too quickly to fluctuation and fatigue. A listener should become so interested in what is being said that they find pleasure in giving their involuntary attention. The ideal training situation exists when both speaker and listener are enjoying maximum pleasure from it.

The trainer should remember that the fluctuation of voluntary attention is largely controlled by the intensity of the stimulus. One of the main reasons for logical arrangement of the training material is to enable the listener to bridge the gaps caused by these attention fluctuations.

It has been found that an increase in the clearness of one idea comes as the result of a fading out of other ideas. In order for one idea to receive its maximum clarity, it must come wholly within the focus of attention at the expense of all the other presented ideas. The number of different objects which can be attended to by the average individual at once is very limited and varies slightly with different sensory types. The general average seems to fall between the range of four to eight seconds.

The reason we have so many confusing presentations from trainers is because they do so much confusing thinking, and their confused thinking is caused by their inability to focus and hold their own attention upon the central idea they are trying to present. The trainer who wants to possess clarity in expression must first obtain clarity in thinking, but they can do this only by developing the ability to bring the central idea into the focus of attention and to hold it there until it is adequately developed and effectively expressed.

Association: Associations are acquired mental connections. When certain parts of a total situation are thought of, other aspects also appear in the focus of consciousness. Thus, if a presentation is arranged in logical order and the main parts of the outline memorized, then the necessary secondary details can be presented without the aid of notes. The main reason so many beginning trainers get confused and fail to remember the important points of their presentation is because they have not established proper connections between the different steps of development within their presentation. During the preparation of a presentation, it is just as important to take the time to establish strong bonds between the main points as it is to analyze and develop those points. It is essential to link adequate bonds between the main points of your presentation, sermon, or teaching materials. It takes adequate preparation to link associated bonds strong enough to overcome stage fright and timidity which beginners experience in front of groups. Some professionals estimate that they spend 6-8 hours of preparation time for each hour of live presentation given in front of groups.

The following classifications of associations are listed to give you a better foundation for applying the principles of association to your training programs. Associations have been classified as *free* and *controlled*. In free association, a person just blurts out any word which presents itself in the thought patterns. A stimulus word is given, and a person starts to speak or write any words which come to their mind. There may be no logical or continuous method in free association. A person experiences free association in all types of dreaming, whether awake or asleep. In controlled association, a person is given a stimulus word and then recalls only the words having a definite relationship to it. In controlled association, words group themselves into certain series, such as opposites, whole-part, part-whole, object-attribute, attribute-object, agent-action, action-agent, genus-species, species-genus, and analogies.

In his book, *The Psychology of Persuasion*, Dr. Kevin Hogan teaches us the Laws of Persuasion. The Law of Association is one of these important laws in the field of business persuasion.

"We tend to like products, services, and ideas that are endorsed by other people we like and respect."

It's a like-like bond or attraction. As well, we see here, the Law of Association now crosses the boundaries of business sales persuasion, over into our study of effective training program development.

There are eight Axioms of Association you need to become familiar with as you develop your training content, teaching materials, and sales presentations. These axioms will give you a basis to help with linking strong bonds of association. These axioms use the inherent principles of both the conscious and subconscious mind to help secure your message not only into the mind of your audience; but also help you with logical recall and delivery of your materials.

1.   The Axiom of Contiguity – experiences that occur together in time or place either successively or simultaneously, tend to be recalled together.

2.   The Axiom of Similarity – experiences which are alike or similar tend to be recalled together, or if one is recalled, it is likely to bring up a similar event or experience.

3.   The Axiom of Contrast – contrasted experiences, or experiences of opposite nature, tend to be recalled together.

4.   The Axiom of Cause and Effect – experiences associated by the bond of cause and effect tend to be recalled together.

5.   The Axiom of Frequency – the more frequently an experience is repeated, the greater tendency for it to be recalled.

6.   The Axiom of Vividness – the more vividly connected experiences are impressed upon the mind, the greater the tendency for them to be recalled together.

7.   The Axiom of Recency – the more recently two experiences are associated together, the more likely one is to recall the other.

8.   The Axiom of Primacy – if two connected experiences are the first of a series, there is a greater tendency for them to be remembered than if they occurred in the middle of a series.

You should capitalize on the various axioms of associations in every conceivable way in order to enable your listener(s) to form strong association bonds between the main points of your training materials. It is not enough for your audience (student, congregation, or client) to be impressed by the presented materials; you must stimulate a movement, purchase, and/or acceptance of your presentation ideas. Your audience should also be able to remember the content of what has been said because of its value and because the method of your presentation was such that they gave favorable involuntary and voluntary attention to it.

The basics of association are of paramount importance to all aspects of speaking, training, and sales presentations. The better you become at mastering the linking fundamentals of association within your materials, the more effective trainer, teacher, speaker, clergy, or salesperson you will become.

Memory: All memory work is largely a matter of habit. Any individual can train their memory to a higher degree of efficiency by properly applying the Axioms of Association. There is a scientific study of memory and association called *Mnemonics*. Further study into mnemonics is suggested if you have the need for intense memorization.

While it is not necessary, nor even suggested to memorize your presentation as a whole, it is important that your outline be organized by a secure network of associative bonds.

If direct memorization needs to occur, such as memorizing a script if you are an actor, the best method consists of the following steps:

1. By the *thorough concentration* on the material to be memorized.

2. By *repetition* of the material to be memorized.

3. By *frequently recalling* the material to be memorized.

The reason most people get the idea that memorization is difficult or impossible for them is because they fail to concentrate on the thing to be learned. During any period of concentration there are other ideas which constantly seek recognition and enter our minds. These extraneous wandering ideas are ignored when the concentration is strong enough on the main centralized ideas, and then those extraneous ideas will just fade from the focus of consciousness.

Repetition is necessary in order to establish the modifications to be made in memorizing a script or an outline. Each time you repeat your materials, you will notice certain parts are more easily memorized than others. It is not necessary to repeat the materials as a whole each time, but to repeat only those parts which you find difficult to remember.

Studies have shown that forgetting is as normal a mental function as remembering. The best assurance against forgetting is to form as many associative connections as possible; once those connections have been established, they then should be tested through the repetition phase to insure their retention.

The most common memory defects are:

➤ Amnesia – inability to acquire or retain mental impressions.

➤ Paramnesia – inability to make proper recognitions.

In developing effective speaking patterns for training programs, your memory, as well as the memory of your audience always recalls, recognizes, and associates past experiences and previously formulated ideas with the current information being presented. It is easy for you as the trainer to keep those previous experiences in check, but you have no control over how audience members will react. Since memory is the retention, recall, and recognition of past experiences; a beginning trainer should always form neutral, non-judgmental memory habits not only within oneself, but more importantly within the mind of your listeners. It is usually difficult to deal with a heckler from the audience once you have activated a judgmental response from them. We will deal with handling hecklers in an upcoming chapter.

Imagination: A trainer who fails to stimulate the imagination of the audience is not speaking effectively. We have discussed the importance of preparation and clear thought in developing your programs, but now we need to make sure you present them in an appealing manner; remembering your appealing manner will change depending on the background of your audience. The function of the imagination is the picturing power of the mind; that constructive and creative faculty which allows us to see a vision of realities that really aren't present under the current existing conditions. The extent to which you stimulate your audience will largely depend upon the vividness of your colorful and playful imagination.

There are two types of imagination:

1.   Productive.

2.   Reproductive.

Productive imagination is the result of putting familiar ideas into new combinations. This form of imagination is useful if you are presenting subject matter which is very familiar to your audience. It shows a great deal of professional ingenuity when you are able to present familiar ideas and facts in a way which allows your audience to catch new meaning from them. Just like re-packaging...putting something old in a new wrapper.

Reproductive imagination is simply the recalling of past images. You must rely on the use of vocal symbols to cause your listener to create or recall mental images. You must take great care in the use of terminology to stimulate the imagination of your audience. There are always several different words which can convey your idea, but it takes time to find just the right one which will spark your listener's imagination. Because of this, you will need to develop a strong vocabulary which includes knowing the subtle differences in the meaning of those words. Online searching in a dictionary and thesaurus, along with using synonyms and antonyms can assist in selecting the most powerful word. Remember that imagination is the process of putting familiar facts into new relationships; being able to paint those vivid pictures in the mind of your listener.

Imagination is an inventive and creative process which involves two steps: presenting the new imaginative idea, and then controlling the response which you have awakened in the listener.

Emotion: An emotion is a type of reaction, or pattern behavior which has been activated in a person. A person's emotional state is an internal reaction from an external force – an external stimulus.

There are various views on the role of emotion as it pertains to speaking; but recent research has shown that emotion is the most powerful trigger to activate within your audience. Emotion plays a critical component in every situation in life, including speaking! A trainer who lacks emotions will never be able to arouse an audience or influence their behavior. To see the power of emotion in action, just watch a Sunday morning television evangelist, and see how they masterfully use emotional tone in their speaking to influence their listeners to send in millions of dollars every week.

Regardless of the type of speaking which you will be doing: teacher, preacher, salesperson, or workplace trainer; in order to be effective, you must arouse some degree of emotion within yourself and within your audience. It takes practice in order to be able to positively control your emotions versus suppress them. An ideal trainer is one who combines strong emotion with clear thinking.

When dealing with people, you'll find one's level of emotional awareness is just as unique as their individual fingerprints. Some people are highly emotional, while others are not able to outwardly show any emotions. You need to be very careful in differentiating between people who have a high degree of control over their emotions versus the person who has suppressed their emotions to a non-existent level.

A normal individual fluctuates between three emotional levels:

1.   The Excited.

2.   The Normal.

3.   The Depressed.

As you speak more and conduct more training programs, you will come to the realization that you cycle between these three emotions during each presentation. You will also discover that as a rule, your audience will react on a corresponding level to your emotional nature combined with the nature of the materials you are presenting at that moment. It is your job as an effective communicator to bring your audience to a level which you deem most advantageous from the standpoint of securing the most desired reactions. For example, if you are training a group of newly hired employees in corporate culture, you will want to make them feel happy, so they will take that attitude into their work environment. On the contrary, if you are conducting an OSHA safety training, then you might want them to feel scared, so they will implement your safety protocols to not get injured.

The nature of the occasion, the content of the training program, the general character of the audience, and your level of experience as a trainer are the factors which determine the emotional level of the audience. Your best audience response is obtained by taking them through rapid changes of the various emotional levels – think of it as an emotional rollercoaster ride. This can only be accomplished when you have complete control over the situation – your content, your emotions, and your delivery.

There are five main theories of emotions:

1.   Plutchik's Theory of Emotion – There are eight basic emotions for all people. They are listed here as a set of four with their contrasting opposites; *joy-sadness, acceptance-disgust, fear-anger, surprise-anticipation.* Plutchik states that each emotion has a possible activating stimulus and a corresponding adaptive behavior. Here is an example for the emotion of fear:

a)   Emotion – *Fear.*

b)   Stimulus - *Any kind of threat or danger.*

c)   Adaptive Behavior - *Protection mode often through freezing (standing still) so you are not noticed.*

2.   James-Lange Theory – Emotion is limited to the consciousness of the individual as a reflex set off by the stimulus. In other words, a stimulus immediately affects the autonomic nervous system and then the message is sent to the brain.

3.   Canon-Bard Theory – A stimulus from a certain event sends a signal which travels to the thalamus, and then it's divided into two signals; one goes to the cortex which triggers the conscious emotional experience of fear, joy, etc.; while the other signal goes to the

hypothalamus which then triggers the physiological changes such as facial expressions and body language.

4. Schachter's Theory - Our environment as well as thought process contribute to the type of emotional experience we have in any situation.

5. Candace Pert Theory - She suggests that emotions take the form of real, concrete substances in our body called peptides. These peptides when released, flow through our body and have a direct effect on body systems. For example, laughter, and the release of endorphins (peptides) which have been shown to have a positive healing effect on the body.

We will leave the discussion of relative merits of these five theories to the psychologists, and just recognize the fact that for planning effective training programs; emotions do exist, and they play a critical role in all of your situations as related to training – both from the standpoint of you, the speaker doing the training, as well as those of the listener in your audience.

> "The world would be a sorry place indeed from an artistic and human standpoint if the distress of the child and of the weak and downtrodden moved no eye to tears. Fame and ambition would be sorry crowns if the multitudes were not moved to acclaim. If all hearers were calm, the great artists would have lived in vain. In a sense, society hangs together because of the possibility of emotional rapprochement." ~ J.B. Watson

Reasoning: Reasoning is the process of forming conclusions, judgments, or inferences from facts or premises. The three factors of reasoning are:

1.   Conception – classification of things.

2.   Judgment – seeing the relationship between things.

3.   Inference – a conclusion from a particular circumstance, a link in the chain of reasoning.

In the process of reasoning, it suggests we have a problem, something which we don't fully understand. The first step in reasoning is to determine the nature of that problem. The next step is to visualize the relationship of the parts to the whole. Then, one must form certain judgments from which we draw inferences. The last step is testing the inferences and then establishing the outcome which is the resolution to that problem.

There are five recognized forms of reasoning:

1.   Deduction – A form of reasoning which consists of drawing conclusions from the general to the specific. A syllogism is the core of deductive reasoning where the conclusion is inferred from two propositions. Deductive reasoning is where facts are determined by combing existing statements. Example:

Premise 1: All humans are mortal.

Premise 2: Oprah is a human.

Conclusion: Oprah is mortal.

2.   Induction – A form of reasoning which consists of the conclusion forming from the particular to the general. Induction is the opposite process from deduction. Inductive reasoning is where facts are determined by repeated observations. Example:

Premise: Up until now, the sun has set in the west every night.

Conclusion: The sun will also set in the west tomorrow.

3.   Abduction – A process of reasoning from effects to (probable) causes. Inductive and abductive reasoning are similar in the fact that both infer the conclusions through repeat observations. Example:

Premise: Every time it rains at night, the grass is wet the following morning.

Conclusion: If the grass is wet, it rained last night.

4.   Analogy – A process of reasoning which infers one particular to another particular. Analogy differs from deduction, induction, and abduction in the fact that it uses two particulars whereas the other three represent a general in one of their premises or conclusions. Analogies play a significant role in problem solving, decision making, perception, memory, and emotion. Other forms of analogy include: examples, comparisons, metaphors, similes, allegories, and parables. The following word examples denote an analogy: *Like and so on, and the like, as if, like.*

5.   Sign – A form of reasoning which consists of assuming that the facts dealt with always, or usually, accompany each other; that the presence of one will be a sign of the presence of the other. Comedian Jeff Foxworthy's noted skits – "You might be a redneck if..," is a comedic use of signs as a form or reasoning. Example:

Premise: Thunder and lightning is a sign of a rainstorm.

Conclusion: When it is thundering and lightening we will get wet from the rain.

Reasoning is a function of the Laws of Thought which is a term given to various principles which govern rational thought. Aristotle first coined that term with these following supporting laws:

a.   The Law of Identity – Each thing is identical with itself.

b.   The Law of Non-contradiction – Each thing cannot both have and not have a given property.

c.   The Law of the Excluded Middle – Each thing either has or does not have a given property.

Gottfried Leibniz, a seventeenth century German philosopher and mathematician later added two additional principles:

a.   The Principle of Sufficient Reason – Things are true for a reason.

b.   The Identity of Indiscernibles – If two things are indiscernible, then they are the same thing.

Arthur Schopenhauer, an eighteenth century German philosopher, expanded on Leibniz's Principle of Sufficient Reason. Schopenhauer added these four cases to support Sufficient Reason:

a.   Judgments about truth are based upon related external judgments.

b.   New states (thoughts) are preceded by existing states (thoughts).

c.   The existence of anything depends on the existence of something else.

d.   There is a reason or 'motive' behind human choices.

The process of logical reasoning enables us to formulate valid judgments. A judgment is reached by becoming aware of the proper relationships between concepts and objects. It is your task as an effective trainer to incorporate as many of these principles of reasoning into your materials as best for the comprehension of your given audience. Each of these tried and true principles have a scientific basis in human behavior. Reasoning is a powerful tool for you to use in all aspects of your life.

Persuasion: Much of verbal and written communication is for the purpose of persuading others to react in the specific manner in which you desire them to react. What is the difference between conviction and persuasion? In the early schools of thought in speaking and business, the salesperson or speaker was instructed to place all emphasis on the attempt to secure conviction from the audience and/or client. In fact, the early development of our education system gave little or no consideration to a student's emotional factors, and even to this day, most public education still doesn't. There are a few exceptions in private education, like the Montessori Method.

Thanks to the field of experimental psychology, we have discovered that throughout a person's entire educational process, one's emotions play an extremely important part at both the conscious and subconscious level. The early sales training of 'brow beating' and 'used car salesmen' conviction sales techniques have been replaced by psychological based persuasion emotional sales techniques. The sad reality, however, is knowing more of this innovative teaching-learning psychology is applied to business settings rather than educating our future leaders within the public education system.

In conviction, we appeal to the intellect, in persuasion, we appeal to the emotions. In conviction we desire to establish belief; our objective is to get the listener (our audience, congregation, student, or client) to believe as we want them to believe. In persuasion we desire to secure action; our objective is to control the listener's response in such a way as to have them react as we desire at the time we desire it.

Although essential, it is not enough for you, as a trainer, to convince your audience as to the truthfulness of your ideas. You must *persuade* them to follow your line of action which you are advocating in your presentation. A listener may be thoroughly convinced that a proposition is a good one, or even that it is the best one, yet they may not be sufficiently persuaded to act in support of what you are proposing. It then becomes your task to use the elements of persuasion, in its various forms, both at the conscious and subconscious levels, until your desired reaction is achieved.

Persuasion can best be achieved by your diligent preparation of knowing your audience, using the appropriate terminology, painting vivid mental illustrations, choosing the correct type of argument, your strength of fervor and degree of personal earnestness that will best be understood, appreciated, and accepted by your listener. In any situation, the audience is persuaded when they react to the stimulus you present in a manner *other* than they would have, had you not applied your particular motivation.

Additional Comments on the Mind

It cannot be stressed enough as to how important this mind dynamics chapter is to your outcome as a successful trainer. You need to commit to ongoing study on the importance of emotions in the selling, educating, and speaking fields. I highly recommend anyone who is in the training profession to study various updated materials on educational psychology.

The old saying of, "sell the sizzle and not the steak," fits for workplace training and speaking, as well as sales. It relates to selling the emotion of the *sizzle* and not the product itself. Your task as an effective trainer, selling ideas and concepts to your audience, is to tap into the imagination of your audience, paint vivid pictures of that emotional sizzle, while persuading them to take your desired actions; keeping in mind that a desired outcome will vary depending on the subject matter and the composition of your audience.

This sounds like a lot of work doesn't it? That is why there are so many mediocre trainers and speakers who don't fully understand and practice the principles detailed in this book. These scientific fundamentals on the power of the mind, coupled with your artistic personality, will produce a winning presentation. This foundational knowledge coupled with practice will elevate you to the status of a *professional* trainer!

Chapter 4

Voice Dynamics

> *"Keep your words soft and tender because tomorrow you may have to eat them."* ~ Unknown

The Mechanics of Speech

The level of attention which you, as a trainer, pay to your voice is very important to our study of training. Every listener has the right to expect and demand that the voice of a speaker be rich in quality, pleasing in pitch, and of adequate intensity. Audiences do not enjoy a presentation given by one whose voice is not pleasing in quality, adequately strong for emphasis and audibility, and agreeably pitched. Listeners give involuntary attention to pleasing voice characteristics, but they find it difficult to give voluntary attention, even for a brief period of time, to voice characteristics which are disagreeable to their ears.

Voice characteristics are the result of training or lack thereof; the same as with any other developmental activity: sports, hobbies, driving an automobile, flying a plane, etc. Vocal sounds depend upon the same fundamental physical principles which are common to all other forms of sound: force, vibration, and resonance. Speech definitely has a physiological basis. We learn to speak in the same manner in which we develop any other useful habit. The psychological steps for all motor learning skills are briefly stated as:

1.   Uncontrolled movement

2.   Accidental success

3.   Repetition of random movements with some degree of control

4.   More success, gradual reduction of uncontrolled movement

5.   Gradual increase of proper coordination

6.   Finally, automatic control of muscles for the proper coordination

The function of speech sounds are produced by body parts which make up a fully functioning vocal mechanism which includes the following four parts:

1.   Motor – The motor consists of the lungs and the respiratory muscles.

2.   Vibrator – The vibrator consists of the vocal cords.

3.   Resonator – The resonator consists of the throat, mouth, and nasal cavities.

4.   Articulator – The articulator consists of the tongue, teeth, lips, hard and soft palates.

All vocal distortions are a result of some physical malformation or malfunction of these vocal components. If there are no physical or habitual defects, your voice will possess pleasing characteristics. Physical defects would include issues such as: deviated septum, cleft palate, tumors, sore throat, abscess/missing tooth, colds, blocked sinus, asthma, or a whole host of other issues that hinder any of the vocal components. A good example of a habitual defect would be a raspy smoker's voice or a stutter.

To utter speech sounds, to vocalize; air is forced from the lungs through the bronchial tubes into the trachea, then through the glottis. The glottis is the opening between your pair of vocal cords. Your vocal cords start to vibrate from the pressure of the air as it escapes the glottis. These vibrations then travel and resonate in the throat, mouth, and nasal chambers. Proper articulation of the vibrations into recognizable sounds and eventually words depend on the proper function of the tongue, teeth, lips, hard and soft palates. Therefore, you can see how important it is to keep all these physical parts of the speech mechanism in proper working order. There are numerous bodily parts required to produce sound, and if any one of them has a defect, it will change your speech patterns, even a single missing tooth!

Your birth cry is the beginning of your vocal career. Look how far you have come since that day!

There are three components to a pleasing voice:

1.   **Pitch** – Pitch refers to the highness or lowness of the voice and is determined by the number of vibrations per unit of time. If you strike the middle C key on a piano, that has 256 vibrations per second and is a good point of reference for speech. A speaker's voice is more pleasing to the ear when their vocal cords are vibrating at less than

256 vps (vibrations per second). One of the main causes for a high-pitched voice, above 256vps, is too much constriction of the muscles controlling the vocal cords. As a professional speaker, you will want to guard against putting excess tension on any muscles which could affect your voice. Even suffering from stage fright and being timid will cause tense muscles and a higher, unpleasing pitch. Most speakers get accustomed to hearing their own voice and many don't know when they have reached a higher tensed pitched. The simple cure for a disagreeably high pitched voice is relaxation and better control of your laryngeal muscles. It is so important for a speaking professional to understand the physiological effects of each component of your vocal mechanism, that way you will have a better idea on how to protect your voice from bad vocal habits or how to repair it if you find some undesirable traits. All control of your vocal cords comes from proper breathing and proper anatomical function of the muscles surrounding the cords. Pitch depends upon the length, thickness, and degree of tension of the cords at the moment of stimulation.

2.   **Intensity** – Intensity refers to the strength or weakness of the voice and is determined by the length of the amplitude of the vibration. When the vocal cords are stimulated by the column of air as it passes through the glottis, the edges swing an equal distance up and down. It is the length of the swing which determines the carrying power of the voice. Pitch has no direct effect upon intensity. A low pitched voice will carry just as far as a higher pitched one. A common vocal misconception is that increased intensity automatically necessitates increased pitch. Many speakers, who have pleasant natural voices, when asked to speak louder, increase their pitch to an unpleasant degree. This can be prevented through the

practice of proper muscle control and breathing techniques. The most crucial point to remember here is that the carrying power of the voice depends entirely on intensity and has no relationship to pitch. In order to properly increase intensity, a speaker must learn to increase tonal support or rib reserve. This can only be done through proper breathing. All of the air taken in by the lungs during inhalation is not expelled during exhalation, but a portion of it is retained. It is this retained portion of air which supplies adequate tonal support from the *rib reserve*. There is a sufficient amount of breath retained in proper breathing, but there is not in improper breathing techniques. A beginning speaker, or one suffering from timidness and stage fright, often loses control over the muscles involved in the inhalation and exhalation processes; even to the extent which their voice becomes jerky. In some cases, the loss of muscle control is so great that it prevents any form of vocalization, such as being *frozen on stage*.

A trainer must clearly understand the principle of harmony among muscles. Muscular control is brought about by one set of muscles acting against another set. For example: if you want to bend forward at the waist, then that act is achieved through voluntary control of one set of muscles. Conversely, if you want to bend backwards at the waist, then that is achieved through voluntary control of a set of muscles which operates opposite from the forward leaning muscle group. Control is established by developing a balanced equilibrium between these two sets of muscles. Adequate breathing is possible only when there is proper operating equilibrium between the muscles which operate in taking air into the lungs and those which operate in expelling it from the lungs, inhaling and exhaling. A professional speaker must practice proper methods of breathing until it becomes an unconscious routine. It should not be necessary to give any thought to your breathing while you are speaking. All of your attention should be focused on the content of *what* you are saying rather than on the mechanics of *how* you are saying it. This applies to breathing as well as to all the elements of vocal delivery.

In order to increase your vocal intensity while speaking, you must increase the force of your breath as it is exhaled through the glottis. Thus, the edges of the vocal cords are set in vibration and the amplitude of their swing is in direct proportion to the force exerted by the column of air. Because you are exerting a higher degree of pressure, you need to be careful not to subject the cords to a sudden shock or strain. Your vocal cords are very delicate in structure and lesions are easily formed on their edges. A huskiness of your voice, either temporarily or permanent, can be caused by lesions. If you breathe properly and do not allow the throat muscles to become too tense, then speaking for many hours can be obtained without any negative fatigue. Speaking stamina, like everything else, comes with many hours of practice. Proper breathing necessitates the expansion of the entire chest and thus why you need to breathe through your mouth. It is impossible to adequately fill your lungs with air by breathing through your nose while speaking. It is OK to breathe through your nose to sustain your life; but for vocalizations, you must breathe through your mouth.

3.   **Quality** – Quality refers to the richness or poorness of a voice and depends upon the number of overtones. The quality is determined by the three

resonating chambers: the throat, mouth, and nasal cavities. The first duty of these resonators is to let the sound come out. Many defective speech patterns result from muffling the sounds in one or more of these resonators. One of the most common types is known as a nasal voice. This comes about from too much or too little air being forced through the nasal chamber during vocalizations. The amount of air is controlled by the free edge of the soft palate.

As sounds pass through a resonating chamber they take on certain characteristics depending on the dimensions and shape of the chamber. It is almost impossible to change the size or position of the throat or nasal chambers, except through injury or surgery, but proper enunciation and articulation requires frequent changes in both size and shape of the mouth chamber. Many people have defective voices because they do not have proper control and relaxation of their lower jaw. Good speakers know how to adjust their mouth chamber to aid in their inflectional needs, thus making sure they don't have faulty resonance. Proper resonance should be accentuated in the front, center, and back regions of the mouth chamber according to the vocal demands of the moment. If there is over-emphasis in the back part of the mouth chamber, then the voice will be husky and blurred; if over-emphasis occurs in the front part of the mouth, then the voice will be shrill and unpleasant.

Nasal resonance is adequate only when it is imperceptible, meaning, neither perceptibly present nor perceptibly absent. Too much air passing through the nose during speech produces a high pitched nasal *twang*. When no air passes through the nasal cavity the voice has a flat twang. All nasal resonance is controlled by the actions of the upper throat muscles and the use of the soft palate. Nasal resonance changes frequently with people who have sinus issues and during the allergy season.

Our cursory discussion here on the components which comprise the speech machine is so you will understand the physics of airflow and vibration for the production of sound. A professional speaker does not need to know an in-depth technical or medical operation of these parts, but just having a basic operational knowledge is essential to help you produce a polished speaking voice.

The first step in correcting voice defects or in the improvement of a normal voice is for a speaker to make an analysis of their current vocal characteristics. Since our ears become accustomed to our own voice, the best method for a proper critique and analysis is to record yourself during a normal speaking situation. When you listen to the playback, you then can become your own critic. By listening to your recording, you can judge your own pitch, intensity, quality, and *nasaliness* of your voice. Once you pinpoint your deficiencies, you then can set out to correct them. It's always good to make frequent recordings of yourself so you can chart your progress and positive changes along your speaking journey.

Seeking Professional Help

You may not have adequate experience to recognize your own deficiencies, nor may you have professional colleagues who can assist in critiquing your recordings. It is my belief that if you are seriously considering speaking and workplace training as a profession, then you should seek a vocal coach/teacher to help polish your voice. The money spent on a couple basic breathing lessons is sure worth the counter-risk of forever injuring your vocal cords. Just Google *vocal coach* in your area to find a list of qualified teachers. Remember, in today's Internet world, it doesn't need to be a coach in your area. The use of Skype, Facebook Live, Zoom, or a host of other online platforms, allows a coach to work with you from anywhere in the world. Also, don't forget to search for free vocal training tips on YouTube!

> **Just as a hammer is a tool for a professional carpenter, so too is the voice for a professional trainer. Always invest in keeping your tools in their proper working order; if not, then injuries will surely occur!**

Vowels, Consonants, and Pronunciation

For the sake of convenience, speech sounds are divided into two classifications – vowels and consonants. You should be familiar with this if you are a fan of watching *Wheel of Fortune!* The element which differs between these two sounds is time. As a general rule, vowel sounds are prolonged slightly, while consonant sounds are spoken more or less instantaneously. Vowels come as a result of an open tone passage, while consonants are momentarily obstructed by the lips, teeth, tongue, hard and soft palates.

Vowels – Vowel sounds are a matter of resonance. The resonating chambers, especially the mouth, take on different shapes according to the needs of the sounds to be produced. Much of the difficulty encountered in diction comes as a result of the speaker's failure to adjust the main resonating chamber, the mouth, to articulate the vocal needs of the moment. Sloppy speech results from inadequate movements and adjustments to the mechanisms of articulation. Vowels are considered short or long according to the character of their individual sounds. Below are examples of the principal vowel sounds which every good speaker must thoroughly understand and practice until their correct sounds become habitual:

> *Long a* (ate)

> *Short a* (add)

> *Long e* (eat)

> *Short e* (bet)

> *Long i* (isle)

> *Short i* (ill)

> *Long o* (ode)

> *Short o* (on)

> *Long u* (unit)

> *Short u* (up)

A speaker striving for good diction and enunciation should practice making the fundamental vowel sounds, while noting the size and position of their mouth. Vowels are formed in three extreme resonances: the front part of the mouth just behind the teeth (*e*), the central part of the mouth (*o*), and the back part (*a*). All of the vowel sounds originate in and emanate from these main resonance positions.

Consonants – Consonants are classified as subtonic (voiced) or atonic (not voiced). With subtonic consonants, the vocal cords experience full vibration, while with atonic consonants there is little if any vibration. Consonants are formed in one of these ways:

➢ Labial - made with the lips. B, W

➢ Linguals - made with the tongue. D, J, L, R, Z

➢ Palatals - made with hard and soft palates. G, Y

➢ Nasal - produced by forcing vocalized air through the nose. M, N

Skill in proper oral delivery for consonants is acquired by studying each individual letter and then in various combinations. Regional speech dialects enunciate consonants differently. For example, if you were raised in the Southern United States, then many people omit the final consonant in certain words. A professional speaker will overcome those learned habits in order to speak with the utmost clarity and technical pronunciation, avoiding regional slurs.

Pronunciation – Good pronunciation comes as a result of proper enunciation of the vowels and the consonants. The two units of pronunciation are the syllable and the sound unit. Pronunciation varies by the region within the country you are born. Those regional differences vary greatly and need to be taken into consideration by speakers who travel worldwide conducting training programs. Oral language patterns are in constant flux and change greatly even within a lifetime. Look back over your life and think of all the changes which have occurred with word usage, and pronunciation, along with the prevalence of slang and texting shortcuts. For a look at greater historical changes, try reading a Bible or Shakespeare! Culturally, a higher educated person is assumed to have proper speaking and word selection. Even with our 21st century worldwide economies and the cultural melting-pot of most countries, education is reflected in one's speech.

> **Speech is the one yardstick by which an individual's degree of cultural development is most often measured.**

Those wanting a professional career in training need to examine their daily speech patterns and re-acquaint themselves with current word usage and pronunciation. Examine, and then improve on your word selection and enunciation, while removing slang and profanity from your daily vocabulary! Continually practice until your proper speech occurs without conscious effort. Only then will you be able to give the necessary attention to the content of your training programs.

Here is a checklist to help develop greater accuracy in pronunciation:

✓ Examine your speech habits carefully to determine whether you have any faults in handling vowels or consonants separately.

✓ Determine whether you have any faults in handling vowels or constants within various word combinations.

✓ Determine which syllable should be given accent.

✓ Determine which letters are to be omitted.

✓   Avoid superfluous sounds.

✓   Prevent the omission of certain syllables.

The above checklist can be reviewed while listening to a recording of your speaking. A recording of your presentation is the best method to master improvements. After a while, your ear will be trained to detect any of the above listed errors.

The best method to learn proper pronunciation of a word is to consult an online dictionary or thesaurus. Each of these resources has the following icon next to every word, and when clicked, the word with proper pronunciation, will be spoken to you. This is a quick and straightforward way for you to improve your speech habits. As a training professional, your speaking ability and speech characteristics will ultimately determine your financial success.

> **Learning correct pronunciation pays dividends, far in excess of the effort it takes.**

Section II: *Dynamic Delivery*

Chapter 5

Body Dynamics

"There are gestures that have a language, hands that have a mouth, fingers that have a voice." ~ Nonnus of Panopolis

Body Language Speaks Louder than Words

This chapter on body dynamics and its use for body language is the ideal chapter to transition from Section I on *Speaking Fundamentals* into Section II on *Dynamic Delivery* techniques. Your body is as important a tool as what we learned your mind and voice are in the previous section. Like your mind and voice, your body has scientific fundamentals which must be mastered prior to delivering a training program, but *how* you use your body starts to reveal the artistic side of your personality.

Bodily action is the most universally accepted method of expression and communication. Whenever a group of people speaking different languages gather, they always resort to some form of bodily expression for the purpose of exchanging ideas. Anyone who has traveled internationally has used body actions to communicate more than trying to speak a foreign language. A head-nod of gratitude, a smile of affection, or glazed eyes of confusion; are the outward expression of inward thoughts and feelings which cannot be adequately expressed with words. The easiest and most effective form of communication is that of body movement and gestures. Any good trainer would be remiss to think that they can adequately express their thoughts and emotions with the use of words alone. The natural counterpart to all vocal expression is that of physical expression. Vocalization is not necessary for action, but action is necessary for adequate vocalization. When Hamlet said, "suit the action to the word, the word to the action…," means for our purposes that when words are used they should be suited to the action and in turn the action should be suited to the words. When your words and your actions are not in unison with each other's true meaning, then your communication is received as phony and deceptive by the audience.

Imperfections in bodily movement are discovered more easily than any other type of faulty technique in speech delivery. Action is the most complete and direct method of expression because it appeals to the eye. A speaker's message is strengthened when they are able to appeal to the audience member's eyes as well as to their ears.

A good speaker knows that their enthusiasm, true purpose, and attitude are all exposed far more through action than through words. It is useless to speak words of interest, concern, eagerness, or sympathy if not supported by identical action. Nothing indicates a mental emptiness as much as does the absence of bodily action. Action is the outward manifestation of an inward conviction, of a strong feeling, or of a combination of these factors.

Effective speaking, whether it is an informal chat with friends, or a formal training session conducted in front of a roomful of strangers requires total, well-coordinated bodily action. A polished professional speaker knows that their body functions as a single unit. When there is a purposeful movement of one body part then there is a coordinated muscle resonance throughout the entire body. Modern psychology and physiology have proven this principle of total bodily integration in each movement. This complete interaction occurs when speaking, in the same manner as if you were dancing, or in any other overt physical activity.

Trainers should bear in mind that every speech situation demands they be alert physically as well as mentally. Science has proven that there is a very high degree of correlation between the two. An active and well-coordinated body is a strong indicator of a keen, vigorous mind. A trainer who suffers from a poorly coordinated and sluggish body usually also suffers from a poorly coordinated and sluggish mind. Speaking is a form of expression involving action, hence effective speaking requires effective action.

Far too many books and training programs are available on the topic of trying to define standardized rules for body action while speaking. Some are good and some are very harmful. Action while speaking cannot be improved by prescribing a set of robotic gestures. The best results for you are from observing your presentations on a video playback; and practicing the congruency between words and movement. The best natural body actions are a result of clear thinking and strong feelings. What looks and feels natural for me might seem forced on you if you used the same movements on the same words and vice versa.

Natural and authentic gestures and expressions have to be congruent throughout your body as a whole.

Usually, the absence of action or the presence of wrong actions can be traced to a lack of understanding or a lack of appreciation of the subject matter. But you are probably asking, "What about inhibitions resulting from timidness or stage fright?" That answer is to select a familiar subject matter and develop your program to the point where your interest in it will produce an internal feeling strong enough to cause you to become so concerned with enthusiastically presenting the content that you will not be self-conscious about anything else; your excitement will drown-out any nervousness or stage fright. Once you develop an inner realization for the value of the material which you are presenting and your obligation to each audience member, any fears or frights will be quickly erased.

The Science of the Body

As a new trainer, you must affirm that there is recognizable bodily language, with every movement visible to your audience members. In order for you to properly develop this language skill, you must consider each division of the physical body and its relationship to the whole.

There are four body divisions that are pertinent to our lessons:

1.   **Trunk** – The trunk is the most important because it serves as the center for the other three divisions. It is also where most of the muscles controlling breathing functions occur. The portion of the trunk which plays the most vital role in body movement is the spine.

Emotional attitudes are revealed more by the action of the spine than by any other body function. A person leans forward in a positive attitude of attraction or leans backwards in a negative attitude of aversion. Everyone leans or bends from their physical center in the trunk. A good trainer is constantly making use of this important gesture of expression; and causes their trunk to respond to the various changes of thought.

2. **Legs** – Your legs act as the agent for motion of the trunk and are an indicator of a speaker's general physical tempo. Your legs reveal your emotional depths and changes in feelings. The movement and position of your legs indicates your determination or lack thereof.

3. **Arms** – Your arms are your agents of contact. They reach out in their eagerness to draw your audience closer so a greater personal connection may exist in a speaking situation. Your arms, just like your legs, reveal the varying attitudes of your mind. They are used to indicate height, depth, breadth, and length. In a defensive gesture, they are used to stop or hold-back undesirable or offensive people as well as thoughts (just like your arms do when you are singing along with the Supremes' song *Stop in The Name of Love*)! Through the *tactile-ness* of your arms and hands they express love, passion, and the tenderness of emotions; in moments of fear and hate they may smash and tear; in moments of grief, they may hang lifeless at your sides; in moments of exhilaration, they may wave happily, and in moments of triumph they may be thrust into the air. The extent of your arm's reach is far and can greatly expand the visual expression of certain points. An effective communicator uses their arms to supplement the expression of ideas through words.

4. **Head** – The head is the accompanying component of all the other parts of the body. For example: if the legs portray strength, then the head is up; if the arms reach out to grasp, the head is eagerly extended; if the spine and chest are relaxed, the head is lowered. In short, the head is the indicator of *total* bodily awareness. The face is the part of the head which serves as the indicator of mental and emotional awareness.

Many speakers are not expressive enough in the delivery of their materials. The main physical component of the body for expressiveness is the eyes. A speaker cannot hope to communicate effectively if they are looking at the ceiling, floor, or walls instead of looking directly at those with whom they are speaking. Eye to eye contact with your listeners is indispensable for all speaking scenarios.

Unanimated speakers will never be heard with a high degree of interest. Animation exhibits itself through bodily action, particularly through general body posture and tension of the facial muscles. The depth of a speaker's conviction for the materials being presented is portrayed to the audience more by the expressiveness of delivery than by the choice of words. If you, as a trainer, are not interested in the subject matter, then neither will your audience!

As a speaker, always remember the interest level in your presentation by your listeners will never be greater than your own personal interest level in it!

The professional trainer assumes all responsibility for presenting their material in such a manner for the audience to grasp its meaning with minimum effort. A lazy or listless speaker cannot expect audience members to fully grasp the content, no matter how worthwhile the materials may be to them personally or professionally. An effective speaker delivers the materials with the utmost precision of all verbal and visual techniques for ease in audience comprehension. Subconsciously, imagine wrapping your key concepts in a gift box and handing it to each audience member.

Beginners Stage Fright and Nervousness

We already touched on this, but it bears repeating. One of the best methods to overcome stage fright and controlling nervousness, besides *really* knowing your subject matter, is bodily action. A beginning trainer needs to practice moving about freely, not random meandering or robotic movements, but with a determined movement which emphasizes the ideas being expressed in words. These movements help to prevent your body from becoming too tense or showing the additional signs of trembling and shaking. A small degree of controlled nervous energy is essential in aiding with animated gestures. Therefore, we will not work on eliminating all nervousness, but focus on its control and proper utilization. A thorough discussion on how to master purposeful body movements is in the next chapter.

The Audience Can Tell

The audience will be grateful to the trainer who has researched in-depth the subject matter and who has familiarized themselves with it, while sufficiently developing techniques to present the materials in an appropriate manner; no matter how dull some required materials may be. Conversely, an audience will typically suffer extreme boredom if a trainer has not thoroughly done their due diligence. The extent to which you master the lessons within this book will be reflected in the eyes and body language of your audience; as well as in your paycheck, booking contracts, and performance evaluations.

Learning To *Read* Body Language

Body language education begins by viewing video playbacks of your presentations as well as watching other  trainers speak. Decoding television interviews of celebrities and politicians will hone your skills in mastering body language. There are numerous body language books available on Amazon as well as YouTube video tutorials. Also, we recommend centerforbodylanguage.com for excellent resources, including a free eCourse. One of the world's top  body language experts is my close friend Tonya Reiman. I suggest her best-selling book *The Power of Body Language*. All of the resources just mentioned will help you establish a solid educational foundation in body language techniques.

Why Is Body Language So Important?

Most of this chapter was dedicated to the scientific understanding of the body and how it interacts and affects the act of speaking. As we mentioned at the beginning of this chapter, physical body comprehension is the *scientific* portion of body language, while your application of body gestures and expressions is the *artistic* portion. Artistic expressiveness reveals your inner personality traits and communicates your commitment to the subject matter being presented. Studying the varying bodily gesture techniques will allow you to further master the artistic applications of body language.

In closing this chapter, I want to revisit the importance of body language as it pertains to speaking and workplace training:

> ❖ **93% of information we receive is non-verbally!**
>
> ❖ **What you *do* is 13 times more informative than what you *say!***
>
> ❖ **Body language doesn't lie or isn't fake like words!**
>
> ❖ **Body language is more influential because it speaks directly to the subconscious mind!**
>
> ❖ **1/30th of a second to make a body language first impression!**

Chapter 6

Proxemics

Esoteric Mind Concepts

Before we can delve into the study of proxemics, we first must discuss additional mind dynamic concepts which were not appropriate for Chapter 3. In Chapter 3, we studied the physical brain and its tangible scientific components which aid in the communication process. Now, we will take the next step and examine mind principles that are not easily locatable, like how the cerebrum is within the brain. Some may say the following discussion is a bit nebulous; but current scientific research is adding validity to these forthcoming mind dynamic concepts which have been present for many millennia in esoteric teachings. Let's comprehend this summarization – the brain is the physical object in your head; while mind is the thoughts created inside the brain. The mind is an esoteric, mysterious component which is harder to describe and cannot be pinpointed as to a specific spot in the brain.

The mind is our consciousness and is the outcome of the operational totality of the brain.

Conceptualize slicing three imaginary horizontal lines through your head to segment the subconscious,

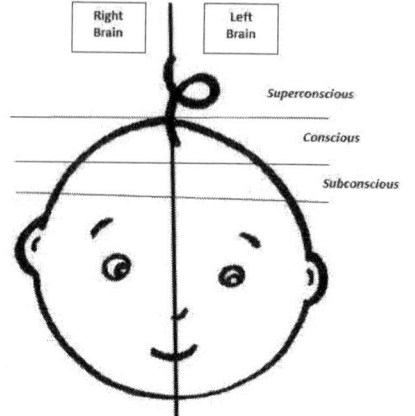

conscious, and superconscious; and then one vertical slice to separate the left brain and right brain. Let's see how these five esoteric theories operate within the realm of consciousness inside the physical brain.

Conscious, Subconscious, and Superconscious Minds

Our conscious mind is the objective computer-like functioning portion. It has no memory capacity; therefore, it's limited to focusing on only one thought at a time. It assesses the incoming information from our five senses of: sight, sound, taste, smell, and touch. The conscious mind continually receives all these sensory inputs and tries to categorize them and determine their relevance; sometimes correctly and sometimes incorrectly. It's the only part of our mind that <u>cannot</u> be trusted.

Our subconscious is like a huge computer hard drive which stores everything that has ever happened to us. It is virtually limitless and never forgets. It communicates through: feelings, emotions, imagination, sensations, and dreams. It operates at a level below the conscious and thus without the knowledge or control of the conscious mind. The subconscious remains hidden from our everyday awareness, but it influences most of what we do each day through the recall of our past memories, actions, beliefs, and habits. This is often why we are unaware of certain behaviors. These functions of the subconscious are vitally important for understanding why body language and proxemics interactions are so critical for a trainer. The subconscious does not produce new creative ideas; it only draws on past influences. A key point to remember is that a majority of the past influences which controls the subconscious are programmed into us through life experiences, mostly from childhood and mostly by parental figures. A must-read book on this conditioning process is *The Four Agreements* by Don Miguel Ruiz.

> **The subconscious is where our *intuition* lives!**

Twentieth-century Theologian Eli Stanley Jones said, "The conscious mind determines the actions, the subconscious mind determines the reactions; and the reactions are just as important as the actions." Here is an example: our conscious mind sees the flames of a fire, and our subconscious tells us not to touch it because it's hot because we have been burnt in the past.

Our superconscious is the mysterious spiritual connection with what some call the God-force or Universal-energy. It is where states of peace, tranquility, and clarity occur during practices such as: prayer, chanting, affirmations, and meditation. The superconscious mind allows humans to be aware of the possibility to achieve greatness, transcend reality, and elevate the human spirit. Intuition and heightened mental clarity are possible because the superconscious sees all things as part of the whole; and is readily able to draw solutions. It sees that problems and solutions are on the same continuum; and summarizes that the solution is a natural outgrowth from the problem. It sees and knows everything from the *50,000 foot view*; it doesn't focus on the individual jigsaw puzzle piece; it sees the completed puzzle from the *above* view.

Some people associate the trinity (three-parts) of consciousness to the Holy Trinity in the Bible where *body* is conscious, *mind* is subconscious, and *spirit* is superconscious. Others use the analogy of an iceberg to describe the three-fold consciousness; where the larger portion under the water level is subconscious, the smaller portion of ice reaching towards the sky above the water line as superconscious, and the rippling water's surface is conscious. Some have the feeling that *Maslow's Hierarchy of Needs*, has a correlation to the three-fold consciousness model; where his basic needs equate to the conscious mind, psychological needs equate to the subconscious mind, and his self-fulfillment needs equates to the superconscious mind. Each of these descriptions is correct; it's whichever one fits best for your level of personal comprehension.

Right-Brain and Left-Brain

The right-brain left-brain theory of dominance suggests each side of the two brain hemispheres controls distinct types of thinking. As we learned in Chapter 3, these two hemispheres communicate with each other by their connecting cord called the corpus callosum. The left hemisphere controls the muscles on the right side of the body and vice versa. This is evident in someone who has had brain damage via trauma or stroke in their right hemisphere and it shows weakened muscle control on the left side of their body. Nobel Prize recipient Dr. Roger W.

Sperry in 1981 studied patients who had their corpus callosum severed and summarized the operational independence of the two hemispheres. Although recent brain research has debunked some of Dr. Sperry's conclusions using updated technology; the latest viewpoint proves that both hemispheres work together in unison and not quite as independent as Dr. Sperry first concluded.

Considerable debate still exists on the esoteric and consciousness level validity to left-brain right-brain-theories. It is still widely discussed that the right-brain is associated with: recognizing faces, expressing, and reading emotions, creating music, appreciating color, using imagination, being intuitive, and being creative. While the left-brain is associated with: language, logic, critical thinking, numbers, and reasoning. As a trainer, communicating and designing curriculum that involves stimulating aspects of both the right and left brains will enhance the comprehension and acceptance of your materials by those with whom you are teaching. Understanding your own strengths and weaknesses as to your right or left brain personal dominance preferences will help you to develop better ways to learn and study; and to communicate.

What is Proxemics?

Proxemics might be a word which most people have not heard of before now. The application of proxemics is crucial to speaking, workplace training, and to communication as a whole. Proxemics techniques and body language techniques work in unison with each other; and both are rooted at the subconscious level of communication. Therefore, their proficiency is paramount to your successful career as a professional trainer.

The field of study called Proxemics was first described in 1963 by cultural anthropologist Edward T. Hall. Proxemics is a division of nonverbal communication which is defined as, "the study of human space and the effects that population density has on behavior, communication, and social interaction." The larger macrocosm of proxemics evaluates the organizational space and layout of houses and buildings, and ultimately the layout of entire cities. The microcosm of proxemics, which we will be examining, deals with human interaction and interpersonal communication as it pertains to our immediate spatial surroundings.

Hall outlined the four classifications of space which surrounds a person as follows:

Intimate Distance: for embracing, touching, or whispering with a distance ranging from less than an inch to 18 inches apart. Sexual intimacy and extremely close friendships are only allowed in this spatial sphere.

Personal Distance: for interactions of close friends and family with a distance ranging from 1½ feet to 4 feet.

Social Distance: for interactions among acquaintances with a distance ranging from 4 feet to 12 feet. Most networking and business interactions occur within this spatial sphere.

Public Distance: used for public speaking with a distance ranging from 12 feet to 25 feet.

We each feel a different sense of ownership for the spaces defined above. Everyone reacts with varying emotional and physical behaviors when these spaces are violated by people who should not be entering them. For example: how would you feel and what would you do if a stranger at a networking event leans in to whisper something in your ear? That would be a breach of your intimate space. Your body language would react with signs of being shocked, startled; and you would immediately want to move away from that individual. Also, your subconscious would form a negative image for that person from then on. You never want to be that negative person who has violated someone's intimate or personal space. For maintaining the best psychological image in the mind of your listeners, you always want to work from the proxemics distance of social and public.

Applied Proxemics and Body Language

A harsh statistic when communicating with people is the fact that at a minimum, 25% of the population was abused as a child; either physical, mental, or sexual. Those memories are locked deep in the subconscious and may be triggered by certain body language gestures from an inexperienced trainer while speaking in-front of an audience. If a trainer awakens any of these deep-seated negative experiences, then the listener will transfer those negative emotions onto the trainer and materials being presented. So here are some dos and don'ts:

➤ **Never** raise your arms above your shoulders. That might trigger memories of being beaten and hit as a child.

➤ **Never** stretch your arms far out to either side of your body. That might trigger memories of being slapped as a child.

➤ **Never** have your hands below your waist in the crotch area. That could trigger memories of childhood sexual abuse.

➤ President Bill Clinton kept his hands and arms within 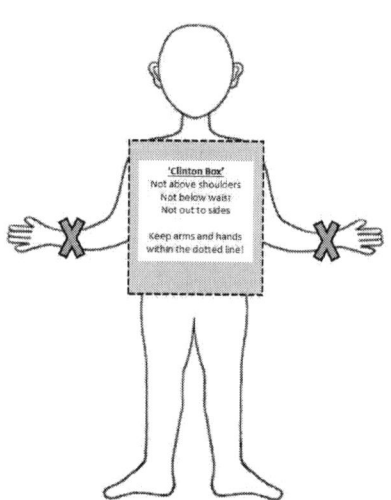 a neutral area on the body when he spoke. Since then, it's been termed the **Clinton Box** for public speaking. When you follow this rule, you will not trigger negative subconscious emotions.

➤ **Never** point your finger at anyone while communicating with them. Finger pointing triggers negative emotions of mother yelling at you for doing something wrong;

it's accusatory. Always gesture with an open hand. Recently, politicians are gesturing with a closed fist while pointing with their thumb. This gesture triggers a sense of power, implying control of the situation.

➢ Mentally define three *emotional zones* on the stage you are working – Neutral, Negative, and Positive. If you are giving neutral information like generic facts, then you stand in your *neutral zone*. If you are talking about negative-emotion information like a downturn in sales, then you stand in the *negative-zone* while speaking those words. If you are talking about positive emotions like giving raises or  a new product launch, then you speak those words from your *positive zone*. It only takes once or twice of you purposefully walking your stage from zone to zone giving the corresponding information for the subconscious of the audience to anchor those emotional responses at that spot on the stage. Then, as you move from zone to zone, your words are amplified by the corresponding emotional response in the minds of your audience. Think of Pavlov's dog salivating at the sound of the bell. You are generating that same stimulus-response reaction by mastering this proxemics technique.

You can arrange these zones in any order of your choosing, but for ease of remembering and consistency, set a defined pattern and use it throughout your entire speaking career. Successful proficiency in this technique is when a trainer effortlessly moves about the stage and stops in the correct zone at the key moment to elicit the corresponding emotional response. There cannot be an obvious march and abrupt stop in a zone; that looks fake and will not have the same subtle subconscious acceptance by the audience.

Movement in front of an audience must look natural and un-intended!

➤ **Beware** of podiums. Most prior encounters with podiums are from teachers, preachers, or politicians; and may have negative connotations. If you are going to use a podium, it is best to use it for neutral factual information. Then, when making deeper emotional connections with the audience, move from behind the podium and stroll over to your positive and negative stage zones.

➤ There is some innovative research being conducted which is reviewing the validity to the concept: about 2/3 of the words and images which enter into the right ear/eye are processed by the left brain; and vice versa, if entered more into the left ear/eye, then about 2/3 processed by the right brain. This

could substantially impact how a listener perceives information. If a speaker wants to bypass someone's emotional filters and go directly to their logical-linear thought patterns, then be slightly off to their right. Conversely, if an emotional response is wanted, then be slightly off to the listeners left side. Further research is occurring on this theory, but it could be a powerful technique in your proxemics tool-bag.

Continual Study

A skillful trainer must constantly re-invest in themselves by learning new computer software and technologies; as well as reading current research reports on educational psychology, training methodologies, public speaking techniques, mind dynamics, brain wave responses, and human interactions. Theories change rapidly on these subjects due to newer research protocols and diagnostic equipment. Some of the concepts in this chapter may have changed by the time you are reading this book. A true professional in any career has an inner motivation for continual learning.

> **"Never become so much of an expert that you stop gaining expertise. View life as a continuous learning experience."**
> ~ Denis Waitley

Section III: *Creative Content*

Chapter 7

Needs Analysis

What is Needs Analysis?

Known as the *father of needs assessment*, Professor Roger Kaufman developed the first model for determining needs within an organization. First coined as a *gap* in results in the mid 1970's, the process matured from gap into *needs*. That maturity took several years and much education in order to change the context of the word *need*, into a noun, instead of a verb; especially, for the fields of educational technology and performance improvement. For our purpose, in the fields of educational psychology and workplace training, one can think of a *need* as a gap (shortcoming) in results which causes negative or unwanted consequences.

A *needs analysis* is a portion of a complete planning process to develop, refine, or improve a product, service, process, or for this book, a workplace training program. By gathering as much information as possible from a variety of sources, you will be able to pinpoint potential problems and have sufficient data to formulate appropriate solutions. A needs process is only effective when they are ends-focused, and they provide hard evidence which can be used to select the best possible means-to-the-ends; based on your organization's budget, desired outcomes, and timeline.

It might help to think of a needs analysis process as your own *Undercover Boss* experience (Yes, the TV show). By watching that TV show, you see how important it is for management to have staff level interactions. The people doing the jobs are the best ones to help with solutions for uncovering and correcting negative issues, not directives by boards or executives!

There are hundreds of journal articles and graphical models one can further educate themselves on this single topic by Googling *needs assessment* or *needs analysis*. You will find a multitude of twelve-step processes taking months or years of assessment and costing millions of dollars. Those might be okay if you are a large multi-national organization or a governmental entity with unlimited budgets; but for the rest of us who cannot afford something that elaborate, I'll will be sharing a few quick low-cost methods in this chapter.

Needs vs Wants

There is an enormous difference between *needs* and *wants*; and that difference is more pronounced when you initiate a process such as this. According to Merriam-Webster Dictionary, a need is a *lack* of means and a want is having a strong *desire* for something. More simply, you *must* have a need (necessity) and you would *like* a want (desire). Needs are limited and may remain constant over time; while wants are unlimited and may change over time.

Needs and wants may shift under a different context. For example, "Is ice cream a need or a want?" Ice cream is a want if you are sitting in your nice house and would like some as dessert; but it becomes a need if you are stranded on an island and haven't had any food or drink for a couple of days. Context is key in all situations, even in developing workplace training programs.

It's important to be diligent in the phrasing of your needs analysis survey questions, making sure to elicit *needs* responses and not *want* responses. However, there is a time and place for both answers depending on your circumstances. If you are looking to develop additional employee benefit programs, more in the soft-skills area, then a *wants* question survey would be fitting.

Questions must be *open-ended* in order to elicit detailed answers. Never use *closed-ended* questions which only require a *yes* or *no* answer; you won't get the necessary results to formulate an effective action plan. Here is the difference:

✓ **Was the last training program effective?** [Closed]

✓ **What are competitors doing that we are not?** [Open]

Once you develop your first needs analysis survey, you can use it as a foundation for all others in the future; by just making minor changes. It is a good exercise for all effective workplace trainers to develop and implement a needs analysis process. The skills and in-depth knowledge you will gain about your organization will surely expedite future programs. Every industry has its own unique challenges, terminology, and procedures; but the process of uncovering gaps which cause unwanted or negative consequences is pretty universal.

Needs Analysis Questions

Below are a few examples of questions which can be used to develop a needs analysis survey (along with a couple wants so you can see the difference). It's important to use the same set of questions for each department in order to maintain consistency if you are searching for organization-wide results. You can develop additional micro-level questions specific to various departments using terminology which defines processes only used within that specific department: HR vs safety vs manufacturing vs sales vs customer service, etc.

Questions like these below allow employees to have an input in the direction of the company and they feel the satisfaction of helping remedy unwanted consequences. If you conduct this as an anonymous survey, then you might receive back more honest results because employees would not feel any chance of retribution.

➤ Identify three (3) of the most time-consuming processes in your department.

➤ Identify three (3) items you think are unique to your department.

➤ Identify three (3) things that you are not doing today, but you want to do.

➤ What is your biggest concern with your department's current procedures?

- Are there any concerns with changing or updating department protocols?

- What represents a successfully operating department to you (please be specific)?

- What additional information do you need to enhance your job performance?

- What report(s) or data do you need to utilize, but do not have the capacity at this time?

- Are there any other issues that you would like to discuss or know more about? [Wants]

- What issues are most critical to your department?

- What new skills would like to learn to enhance your professional and personal life? [Wants]

- What are the competitors doing that we are not?

- What do you like best about our products or services?

- What do you like least about our products or services?

- What should we do to improve our customer satisfaction?

- In the past few months, what was the smallest change made in your department that had the biggest positive result?

➢ Are we as a company changing as fast as our industry around us? If not, then what do we need to do?

➢ What specifically can your manager do to better support your team's mission?

➢ What stupid rule needs to be abolished?

➢ Does our company or organization represent a high-quality product, mission, or service? Explain.

Learning and Development or Workplace Training, whichever terminology you use, can also be considered an employee benefit by teaching skills your staff can use not only at work, but also in their personal lives. Questions like these above allow you, as a trainer, to maintain a priority list of additional skills which you can develop into programs that are of interest (wants) to your staff. Training programs also have an impact on employee retention by allowing good employees to feel valued, while learning new skills; especially when they have a voice in the process of which programs your training department teaches.

Needs Analysis Sampling Size

There are two basic formats of needs assessments: extensive and intensive. The difference is the size of the groups who will be surveyed to gather the data for your analysis. An extensive sampling uses a large number of cases or individuals, while an intensive sampling uses a fewer number. Here is how to categorize the difference:

Extensive vs	Intensive
General Public	All Your Employees
All Your Employees	Employees Within A Specific Department
Employees Within A Specific Department	A Few Key Employees Within A Department
All Your Employees	A Few Key Employees Within Each Department

Extensive assessments typically are more expensive and more time consuming to conduct, but you receive a broader range of feedback data from a larger cross-section of your sampling group. Intensive assessments would be quicker and less expensive to conduct, and your results would be more focused to pinpoint exact needs. There is a time and place for both of these assessments based on your desired outcome.

A **public hearing** is a formal meeting of the general public to receive testimony (data) on important proposed issues. Public hearings are great tools to conduct extensive needs assessments. Opposing views are vocal at public hearings and order must be maintained to focus discussions to receive useful data.

A **strategic planning session** is an organization's process for defining strategy, direction, and setting priorities. These are typically comprised of department heads and/or upper management. They would be a good place to conduct an intensive needs assessment.

A **focus group** is a small, but demographically diverse group of people gathered to observe reactions on a particular issue. Focus groups are generally used in market research and new product releases and would be an intensive needs assessment classification.

If time and budgets permit, it might be advantageous to conduct both intensive and extensive needs assessment processes and compare the results; especially if you are dealing with a paramount life-changing issue within your organization. However, for most cases involving workplace training, an intensive needs process is sufficient.

SWOT

A SWOT Analysis is a really simple but powerful tool which helps define business strategy. SWOT stands for *Strengths, Weaknesses, Opportunities,* and *Threats*. Some use a SWOT Analysis as a unique stand-alone extensive needs assessment by asking the survey group these four questions:

What are the organization's (or the issue) strengths?

What are the organization's (or the issue) weaknesses?

What are the organization's (or the issue) opportunities?

What are the organization's (or the issue) threats?

Strengths and weaknesses are internal to an organization, those things over which you have some control and can change: your team members, intellectual property, patents, and processes. Opportunities and threats are external to your organization, those things which you mostly have no control: competitors, price of raw materials, or consumer trends. A savvy organization is able to take advantage of opportunities and protect against threats, but you cannot change them.

SWOT		ANALYSIS	
S	Strength #1 Strength #2 Strength #3	**W**	Weakness #1 Weakness #2 Weakness #3
O	Opportunity #1 Opportunity #2 Opportunity #3	**T**	Threat #1 Threat#2 Threat #3

Once you have designed your needs assessment survey and collected everyone's input, now what do you do with all the data? A SWOT chart is a perfect structure to organize the data received from any form of needs assessment: extensive or intensive; employee survey, or public hearing, or strategic planning, or focus group. A SWOT chart adds additional inputs for analysis instead of using a basic two-column (negatives and positives) T-chart. By distilling your data into a SWOT (or T) chart, you can easily compare your data to formulate the best response to address your gap; the unwanted or negative consequence which originally initiated the needs assessment process.

Sources to Develop Programs

There are many sources at your disposal which you can use to help develop workplace *needs* and *wants* training programs, surveying your employees or staff is just one of these sources. Let's look at other possible resources for program ideas and content:

➤ CEO / Executive Director / Senior Management – Senior staff is an excellent resource for training topics, program goals, and content ideas. They are in those positions because of their previous workplace experiences and bring with them a wealth of knowledge. They may also mandate specific training topics for the overall benefit and direction of the entire organization.

➢ <u>Board of Directors</u> – Many people forget about the untapped knowledge which board members bring to the organization as a whole. Typically, they are involved in other businesses within the community and have access to varying resources within other market segments. Private meetings with individual board members or a generic needs analysis survey for all board members are a couple of ways to garner useful information from these knowledgeable individuals.

➢ <u>Government Regulatory Agencies</u> – Depending on your industry, there might be mandated government training protocols you are required to teach. Some may be specific to certain departments, and some may be company or organization wide. Most of these are usually health and safety related programs.

➢ <u>Insurance Company</u> – Many people forget to check with their liability insurance company. Depending on your industry, your insurance premiums could be lowered if you maintain documented staff training. If your staff (or a certain percentage of your staff) is trained on topics like CPR, first aid, safety protocols, infectious diseases, conflict of interest, ethics and standards, or others; then you could see a reduction in your liability premiums.

➢ <u>Poach Your Competitors</u> – If there is any way to get a copy of the training curriculum from your competitors, then you could tweak their content to fit your needs. This book is not promoting you go out and steal these materials, but maybe you have a current employee who previously worked at a competitor and would share those materials.

- ➤ <u>Software Developer</u> – There could be various software systems in place at your organization which require employee training. The developer of the software is a great resource for generic materials which you can enhance by customizing for the exact implementation; based on your policies and procedures for each department.

- ➤ <u>External Stakeholders</u> – Depending on your industry, you may have external influences which will need input on the development of your training programs. Examples of external stakeholders include suppliers, customers, software user-groups, affiliated nonprofit organizations, other government agencies, or maybe even the general public.

- ➤ <u>Old Programs</u> – Recycle old materials. Go through the archives of your organization and look at old training programs. You will probably have to update them to meet newer standards or technologies; but enhancing something old is a lot less effort than starting from nothing!

- ➤ <u>Legal Staff</u> – If you work for a large corporate or government entity, then legal staff may have to review your training materials. Also, the legal staff might direct you to develop and conduct training on changes to the law, updated or new usage of forms, or policy changes.

Accreditation

The results you uncover through your needs analysis process will help you define the direction of your programs as to CEU approved or certificate granting. There is a significant difference between programs which earn CEU /

CEC's (Continuing Education Units or Credits), and other programs that just offer a participatory certificate for course completion. Much thought has to be given as to which of these two directions each of your courses will be designed to address. It mostly depends on who your audience is; if they belong to professional organizations requiring yearly refresher courses, and then you will want to examine how to grant CEU's. If your audience is the general public or this is a soft-skills knowledge program, then giving a certificate at the completion of the course is satisfactory.

Psychologically, there is a sense of reward and purpose when someone receives a certificate after completing a course. It may allow them to add it as a resume item and proudly display a certificate in their cubicles. *Always* give some type of certificate for the attendees of your programs, even if it is just a printed one from Microsoft Word or Publisher.

Being able to grant CEU's can be an extensive accreditation process, depending on the organization(s) from which you are requesting authorization. Professional licensing boards and organizations have a rigorous process to not only approve the content of your curriculum, but also the qualifications of the instructors. Usually, this involves FBI fingerprint background checks for authorized instructors.

Let's look at a few examples of different industries and brainstorm on where you could get accredited to grant CEU's:

- Medical related – Your state's board of medicine, dental, pharmacy, or nursing; and nationally, the boards for medical assistants.

- Beauty related – Your state's board of cosmetology.

- Mental health or social services related – Your state's board of psychology or social work.

- Safety related – Your state's board on workplace health and safety; or even nationally, OSHA.

- Union audience – Each various union your participants belong to.

- Real Estate – Your state's board of realtors.

- Automotive – Your state's department of motor vehicles or mechanic licensing board.

- Teachers – your state's board of education or even your local school district.

- Business – Your state's board of accountants, auditors, or bankers; nationally, various business organizations.

- Children – Your state's board of education. In some states, daycare and childcare establishments may fall under a different statewide accreditation organization.

- Nonprofits – If you are a nonprofit in one of the market segments already mentioned, then start there. If not, your state may have an alliance for mentoring all nonprofits.

These are just a few ideas for you to consider contacting for CEU accreditation. Your organization might have several training programs which are approved by one or a combination of different accrediting sources. It will be up to you as the workplace trainer to make sure you adhere to the curriculum requirements for each source you are authorized to grant CEU's. Many sources require a yearly re-review of curriculum and training staff, so be prepared to maintain proper documentation. It is quite prestigious to list on your training resume that you are a CEU granting instructor with the State of X's board of Y.

Be creative with your search for opportunities to get your training programs CEU authorized. Remembering you may have resources at the city, county, state, and national levels.

Chapter 8

Content Design

> **"Tell me and I forget, teach me and I may remember, involve me and I learn."** ~ Benjamin Franklin

The first question you will be asked in a job interview for a trainer position is, "What do you know about adult learning theories?" This question leads to ponder the premise that adults learn differently than children. But is it really true? This premise then leads to the second question, how different is workplace training from academic teaching? Let's look at these two questions and see how they should impact designing your training programs.

Workplace vs Academic Training

In Chapter1, we touched on the differences between a teacher, speaker, and trainer. Now, let's look at the similarities and differences between workplace learning vs academic learning. The two biggest differences between an academic college course and a workplace training seminar seem to be *time* and *intent*.

Workplace training is intended to teach employees a new or updated skill which will be beneficial for them in their work lives. Academic training is for people who want to gain a more general knowledge, certification, or degree.

Sometimes an academic student intends to use their new knowledge in their career, and sometimes they don't. Education for education's sake vs education for an implementable skill is another way to differentiate the two modes of learning.

Time is a major factor in these two classifications of learning, which causes a direct impact on the content of the subject. For example, a three credit college course typically meets for three hours once a week for 12 to 15 weeks; therefore, 36 to 45 hours of class time; plus, additional homework. But in a workplace environment, you are lucky to have a seven hour day of training; most likely you will have only 2 to 4 hours of instruction time.

Because of this vast reduction in time for instruction, academic courses are structured differently than workplace courses. Academic curriculum has the luxury to explore multiple viewpoints on the subject as well as examples and discussion time. While workplace training has to be laser focused and only deal with the direct application of the subject as it pertains to each employee. You don't receive a well-rounded or detailed view of the subject; only a 'down and dirty' view that must align with management goals.

As a trainer, it's crucial your training message aligns with the corporate culture and a lot of the time, the political and social leanings of the CEO. Sometimes this is a slanted bias, but that is your job, to train the curriculum based on who is paying you.

Both of these classifications of learning are to expand the knowledge base of class participants, but each has a different methodology. You will find, a lot of the time, workplace training presents more current updated information and build upon the foundational knowledge which people have acquired in their previous academic degrees. Therefore, shorter class times are manageable because students already have either previous knowledge or years of practical applications of the subject. This chapter will educate you on multiple learning theories to help hone your teaching skills for a variety of situations.

Adult vs Children Learning

Just as the difference between workplace and academic training can be distilled down to time and intent; the difference between adult and child learning can be distilled down to *discipline* and *motivation*. Broadly speaking, children are *forced* to learn in elementary through high school, while adults *choose* to learn in college and the workplace. The free-will choice and willingness to learn as an adult expedites the learning process.

Discipline and bad behaviors are present in both adult and child learning scenarios; and sometimes they are even worse with adults! The adult ego is very powerful and the most difficult training behaviors arise when an adult is trying to *grandstand* and *show-up* the instructor by showing the rest of the class how much they think they know about the subject. It's hard to give a disruptive adult a *time-out* in the corner or have Sister Antonia smack their knuckles with a ruler!

The debate on the differences between adult and children learning has been going on for decades. In 1970, Dr. Malcolm Knowles in his book *The Modern Practice of Adult Education: Andragogy Versus Pedagogy*, fostered this divide. Dr. Knowles popularized the words *pedagogy* and *andragogy*. Where pedagogy means teacher-focused learning (child) and andragogy means learner-focused learning (adult). He summarized these five points of difference:

1. **Learner** – Adults are independent and want autonomy to choose for them self. Children are dependent on rules and the instruction of the teacher. Adults have grown-up and don't want to go back to that dependent feeling.

2. **Experience** – Kids have little to no experience with the learning subject. This usually makes them slightly more attentive and willing to listen to the teacher. Kids look for role models to help with development; while adults usually have a wealth of experiences which form their biases on the subject.

3. **Readiness** – Kids progress through levels of learning; kindergarten through twelfth grade in the USA. It's a building process and their teachers assess whether they are ready to graduate to the next level, or not. Adults are guided by their own want/need to learn. If an adult feels there is a lack in their education, they are motivated internally to search for resources.

4. **Perspective** – Adults see learning as a means to solve an existing issue. Kids have not developed a conscious sense to know why the subject is, or will be, important in their lives.

5. **Motivation** – Adults are motivated to learn by emotions and aspirations to make their lives better.

This is an internal motivation. Kids are mostly motivated by external forces like: competition, peer pressure, fears of failure, and parental force.

Remembering the lessons in Chapter 3 on *Mind Dynamics*, plus what we just learned in this section, this whole *hoopla* on adult learning theories in workplace training has no basis from the physical mechanics of the brain and learning. It is more a factor of appeasing adults on their previous experiences, allowing choice versus cramming education upon them like a child, and making them know ahead of time *why* it is important for them to learn this material. Thus, the secret to workplace training:

> **"Foster a classroom environment such that the participants feel it is their choice to listen and learn from you; while they *perceive* you respect and value their attendance!"**

Bloom's Taxonomy

In 1956, Benjamin Bloom and his colleagues published *Taxonomy of Educational Objectives*, which was a framework to categorize academic educational goals for K-12 teachers and college instructors. This framework is more commonly known as *Bloom's Taxonomy*. Bloom and his co-authors designed a system of six categories: Knowledge, Comprehension, Application, Analysis, Synthesis, and Evaluation, where knowledge is the requisite for the other five skills/abilities.

Bloom's Taxonomy developed a simple roadmap to learning with an underlying message stating, "learning is the ability to create something new." In 2001, a group of psychologists, theorists, and researchers revised Bloom's original work and called it *A Taxonomy for Teaching, Learning, and Assessment*. They changed the original six categories from nouns to verbs, and relabeled them with the following meanings:

> **Remember** – Recognizing and recalling information. They thought this was paramount because each of the following additional five abilities are based on remembering information. Simply memorizing information is the lowest level of learning, and learning expands and blossoms as you proceed through each of the next levels.

> **Understand** – Interpreting, exemplifying, classifying, summarizing, inferring, comparing, and explaining comprise the next level of learning.

> **Apply** – Executing and implementing.

> **Evaluate** – Checking and critiquing.

> **Create** – Generating, planning, and producing.

You see, as we progress through each step from remember to create, our depth of comprehension and awareness has to increase of the subject matter. Just like going from first grade to fifth grade. This is the same *Readiness* process that Dr. Knowles explained.

This 2001 update also defined *knowledge* as four different sub-sets:

> **Factual Knowledge** – terminology; specific details and elements.

➢ **Conceptual Knowledge** – classifications and categories; principles and generalizations; theories, models, and structures.

➢ **Procedural Knowledge** – subject-specific skills and algorithms; subject-specific techniques and methods; criteria for determining when to use appropriate procedures.

➢ **Metacognitive Knowledge** – strategic knowledge; contextual and conditional use of cognitive tasks; self-knowledge.

An interesting point which workplace trainers must remember is they usually don't know the baseline knowledge level of the people in their classes. Unlike a college professor who might teach Statistics 301, and who knows each student has the foundation of knowing the material from the prerequisite courses of Stats 101 and 201. A workplace trainer will find it very useful to implement the steps of Bloom's Taxonomy to their content, even if just for a quick preliminary review of the information; so, everyone will feel comfortable with your starting point.

Learning Styles

People learn through three broad categories:

1. Visual Learning (seeing)

2. Auditory Learning (hearing)

3. Kinesthetic Learning (touch/feel)

Many researchers and educators have expanded on, redefined, and categorized these three foundational ways of learning to try and enhance countless frameworks to explain learning. Whether they are called: theories, modes, intelligences, aptitudes, styles, or categories; each can be beneficial in the academic and workplace learning environment. In fact, all of them are rooted in academic education, but we will look at several of them which are useful in designing workplace course content.

Gardner's Multiple Intelligences

In 1983, Dr. Howard Gardner from Harvard University and his colleagues published the book *Frames of Mind: The Theory of Multiple Intelligences*, which first proposed the notion that people learn in ways more than those original three. Gardner has since expanded on his original *Intelligences,* and below are the current nine. I have added related jobs to each one, so you begin to see how your training should be designed based on your audience:

1. **Verbal-linguistic**. Well-developed verbal skills with sensitivity to the sounds, meanings, and rhythms of words. Teachers, trainers, speakers, sales, and journalists are a few of the job listings for this type of person.

2. **Logical-mathematical**. Ability to think conceptually and abstractly, with a capacity to discern logical and numerical patterns. Jobs would be: engineer, pilot, scientist, math professors, physicist, or astronaut.

3. **Spatial-visual**. Capacity to think in images and pictures, to visualize accurately and abstractly.

People who tend to be interior designer, architect, artist, detective, or photographer would work with these intelligences.

4. **Bodily-kinesthetic**. Ability to control one's body movements and to handle objects skillfully. Pro sports players, dancers, choreographers, and acrobats would be proficient in bodily-kinesthetic intelligence.

5. **Musical**. Ability to produce and appreciate rhythm, pitch, and timber. These jobs would be singers, composers, orchestra conductor, and musicians.

6. **Interpersonal**. Capacity to detect and respond appropriately to the moods, motivations, and desires of others. Social worker, therapist, and a mother!

7. **Intrapersonal**. Capacity to be self-aware and in tune with inner feelings, values, beliefs and thinking processes. Fiction writer, poet, illustrator, chef, and psychologist.

8. **Naturalist**. Ability to recognize and categorize plants, animals, and other objects in nature. Botany, horticulture, zookeeper, and park ranger would be a couple jobs.

9. **Existential**. Sensitivity and capacity to tackle deep questions about human existence. Minister, monk, guru, and philosophers would have an affinity to this intelligence.

Although the added job types to each intelligence was just to get your mind thinking, each profession has multiple cross-over intelligences. For example: A good surgeon must be proficient in verbal-linguistic, logical-mathematical, interpersonal, spatial-visual, bodily-kinesthetic, and intrapersonal skills.

You can use these intelligences for curriculum development, planning instructions, selecting course activities, and developing assessment strategies. Gardner says, "...regardless of which subject you teach: the arts, the sciences, history, or math; you should present learning materials in multiple ways." So how can you apply these theories to improve your training?

- ✓ Project your content on a screen and/or have printed handouts for the visual learners.

- ✓ Speak your content so the verbal people can hear your message.

- ✓ Have graphs or charts in various parts of the room so people have to spatially look around; or a puzzle of your content which people have to assemble.

- ✓ Have small activities and 'icebreakers' (Chapter 12), so people have to bodily move about the room.

- ✓ Design small group, break-out sessions where people have to assess and discuss the interpersonal and intrapersonal aspects of your content (Chapter 10).

This was a quick example on how to harness the power of Gardner's Multiple Intelligence theory which will bring about increased comprehension, acceptance, and awareness of your materials by playing to the strengths of various people's learning aptitudes.

Montessori Method

When the word *Montessori* education is heard, most people jump to the conclusion of white-privilege and high priced private schools. Unfortunately, what the teaching method has morphed into is a direct opposite of its founder Dr. Maria Montessori. Dr. Montessori developed this unique teaching system in 1907 in Italy, as a way to educate disenfranchised special needs children with intellectual and developmental disabilities. She believed children learn better when they choose what to learn. An article from 2006 in *The Journal of Science* concluded that Montessori students have an edge over traditional public school students in both academic and social development.

Here is what makes the Montessori Method so different:

> ➤ Mixed ages. Classrooms are mixed in ages and grade levels. Older students get to mentor younger ones, and younger ones become inquisitive on what their older role models are doing.

> ➤ Same teacher. Montessori teachers stay with a group of students for several years, they don't change each grade year. This allows teachers to have deeper connections with students. Teachers are able to focus on the whole student: social, emotional, intellectual, and physical development are better assessed; allowing the teacher to be proactive with any developmental changes they may see.

> ➤ No linear desks. A Montessori classroom does not have traditional rows of desks with a stark delineation of students in seats and teacher at the

front of room. These rooms are made-up of various activity stations scattered around and teachers move amongst students, no front versus back.

➤ No traditional grades. Traditional grading scales do not exist. A student's progress and achievement are based on their aptitude instead of letter grades. Naysayers contend that this does not foster competitiveness amongst youth.

➤ Hands-on. Montessori learning is based on independent hands-on learning. The various workstations are designed for interaction with concepts pertaining to the lesson and students work on differing projects to comprehend the lesson as a whole.

➤ Unique teaching aids. This is a major component as to why Montessori education is so expensive. They spend a fortune on unique customized teaching aids that are bright, colorful, and tactile for learning the lessons.

➤ Beautiful environment. Classrooms are beautiful: open, airy, with lots of natural sunlight. This fosters a positive learning environment for independent study.

Students who are educated in a Montessori environment tend to be able to manage themselves and think independently, thus why so many artists and entrepreneurs are graduates. Names like: Sean 'P. Diddy' Combs, Julia Childs, Anne Frank, Amazon CEO Jeff Bezos, along with Google founders Larry Page and Sergey Brin are just a few notable alumni.

What are some ways to incorporate Montessori techniques into workplace training?

✓ Custom build teaching aids to enhance your message; making sure they are colorful and tactile.

✓ Arrange your room for small group tables or pods, and you as the instructor move about the room instead of being stationary in the front.

✓ Hold your training in locations that are different than a traditional meeting room or auditorium. Maybe outdoors surrounded with nature and beauty.

✓ Interactions. Design your content for more interaction instead of traditional verbal or reading instruction.

As we examined these unique points to Montessori teaching, it seems as if it is a culmination of all the good points from Gardner's Multiple Intelligences and Bloom's Taxonomy; along with the attributes on how to instruct adults versus children. It's as if Montessori is treating kids like little adults! What an interesting concept!

VARK

After spending thousands of hours of classroom observations, Neil Fleming and Coleen Mills created the VARK Learning Style in 1992. VARK stands for: **V**isual, **A**uditory, **R**ead/Write, and **K**inesthetic. The interesting point here is that they really didn't discover anything new; we already know that visual, auditory, and kinesthetic learning has been around since the beginning of humankind. Some will argue their Read/Write style is really not its' own unique style; but a factor of the other three. And, comparing this to Dr. Montessori's breakthrough learning style over 80 years prior; this is really stepping backwards in learning theories.

However, what they did do which has enhanced educational theory, is categorize actionable learning strategies for each of the four learning modes. For example, to enhance content delivery for Visual learners, you should:

✓ Be creative with charts, diagrams, mind maps

✓ Create flashcards

✓ Color-code, underline, and /or highlight information

In the *Resource Section*, we have a direct link to dozens of other VARK learning strategies to enhance your training methods for each of these four learning modes.

4MAT

Dr. Bernice McCarthy developed the 4MAT structure in the late 1970s. She was a kindergarten teacher and became enthralled with the diverse ways children learn. This model has a right-mode and left-mode strategy which is in direct correlation to the right-brain and left-brain uniqueness we learned in Chapters 3 and 6.

The 4MAT model has four quadrants, each with a unique question, and then a strategy for left and right comprehension:

Meaning   Why?   Connect / Attend

Concepts	What?	Inform / Image
Skills	How?	Extend / Practice
Adaption	If?	Refine / Perform

In the *Resource Section*, there is a link to the 4MAT visual model with implementation ideas for workplace education.

Spaced Repetition

Spaced repletion is an evidence-based learning technique founded on the German 1970's Leitner System. Spaced repetition is also known as: spaced rehearsal, expanding rehearsal, graduated intervals, repetition spacing, repetition scheduling, spaced retrieval, and expanded retrieval. It is a technique usually performed with flashcards and was developed to improve long-term memory in young children trying to learn new concepts and also older individuals with Alzheimer and dementia issues.

This technique works by newly introduced and more difficult flashcards are shown more frequently, while older less difficult flashcards are shown less frequently in order to exploit the psychological spacing effect. This has been proven to increase the rate of learning and is beneficial with mathematical formulas, scientific equations, and learning a new language. Designing spaced repetition flashcards would be ideal for health and safety applications, along with memorizing complex technical workplace information.

Generational Concerns

As of the writing of this book in 2023, we have the most diverse workforce, with people working longer in their lifetime, and the greatest number of generations co-mingling in the workplace. Each generation has its own unique qualities which a trainer must contend with while training:

> **Matures aka Traditionalists**: born 1909 – 1945. Grew up during the Great Depression and World War II. Values quality over speed. Driven by ideals of duty, sacrifice, and loyalty.

> **Baby Boomers**: born 1946 – 1964. The 'Me' generation. Focused on prosperity, status, and individuality. Works well in a team.

> **Gen X**: born 1965 – 1980. Embraces technology. Loyal to people, not companies. Dislikes hierarchies, and questions authority.

> **Millennials**: born 1981 – 2000. Extremely tech-savvy. Coddled and protected from birth. Considers global impact on issues. Seeks open, constant communication. Torn between a desire for individuality and the need to fit in.

> **Gen Z**: born 2001 – 2020. Technology completely controls their life. Entrepreneurial driven. Lonely and depressed. Decreased interest and belief in religion.

These generational attributes cause much strife for trainers. It's difficult to design a program with appropriate content in a manner which addresses each of these above unique points. As we have said, it's crucial to know the make-up of your audience and the proportion of each of these age groups. Having a cursory knowledge of these generational differences at least gives you a footing to begin a discussion on trust and understanding.

Even in your open remarks for your program, if you say, "I acknowledge the generational diversity in the room and know everyone has different values and learning styles; I will do my best to respect those differences. I will also explain the concepts in multiple ways to enhance your comprehension." An opening statement such as that will gain you immense respect, right from the beginning! But the deeper level of understanding for you is to grasp that the more strategies you embed into your curriculum from the multiple learning theories from this chapter, the greater chance you have to satisfy these generational attributes.

Traditional Content Structure

You learned how to deliver a presentation back in middle school and high school. Remember those dreaded book reports or nerve-racking public speaking exercises? But look at you now; a polished professional who will be paid big bucks to train large groups of people! Let's review the concepts of designing a traditional presentation:

Opening – Catch Their Attention

⊓ A startling question or challenging statement.

⊓ An appropriate quote, illustration, or story.

⊓ Display an appropriate object or picture.

- A generalization which focuses attention and ties in with your subject.

Body – Support Your Purpose

- The body of your presentation contains the factual support for your purpose. The amount of information you can include in the body will be limited by the amount of time available. The type of information will depend on your training goals and style. The body main contain: research, proof, evidence, fact, figure, statistic, definition, example, illustration, anecdote, authority, and/or analogy.

Conclusion – Bring It All Together

- A summary of the points you have made and the conclusions to be drawn from them.

- A specific appeal for action.

- A story, quotation, or illustration to emphasize your points.

When designing a professional workplace training program, it's crucial to be more thorough and creative than just this basic presentation structure. One thing we can incorporate into content design from the study of persuasion and influence is the phenomenon of sequencing. Sequencing teaches us, "the first shall be last and the last shall be first!" Meaning, in the majority of circumstances, the points you mention last in your program are not only the main points people will remember first, but will be the item they first act on. The second most popular choice or importance ranking is the point you mentioned first.

Therefore, hold the most crucial point until the very end, but open with your second most important or powerful point. All other supporting content is sandwiched between the first and last points. Your supporting points outline would look this: **2**, 3, 4, 5, **1**. By harnessing the power of psychological sequencing, you will gain a higher rate of compliance from your audience, while being perceived as a more dynamic and effective trainer!

Learning Barriers

Pre-planning on your part and taking into consideration all things which may negatively affect your presentation are part of the job as a professional. Let's examine the most common barriers which derail a smooth training program:

> **Environment** – environmental concerns can be inside and outside. Will the weather outside impact your program? Will storms cause participants to arrive late? Is your meeting location easily accessible to parking lots? Is your location easy to find and on a main road? If not, you need to provide detailed maps and written directions on how to find the location. You have no control over last minute rain or snowstorms and may need to delay the start of your programs if Mother Nature is not cooperating. Is the inside temperature of the room conducive to learning? Too hot or humid will cause people to be sluggish or fall asleep, and too cold will have participants shivering and not paying attention. It is always best to have the temperature of the room a couple of degrees on the cooler side and forewarn participants to bring a sweater or light jacket.

➢ **Handicap** – will you have handicap participants attending? Is the location of your class easily accessible for wheelchairs, walkers, and crutches? Do you have special seating set aside to accommodate these attendees?

➢ **Blind or Deaf** – do you have seating in the front of room for people hard of hearing or with diminished eyesight? Try to place people with hearing difficulties near a speaker so they can hear better. Do you need a sign language interrupter to *sign* your presentation? Do you have special seating and outdoor access if there is a seeing-eye dog in your class? Will you be projecting your presentation on a large screen so people in the back rows can easily see your materials? Likewise, will you be using a microphone and speakers so everyone can clearly hear you? Will you need to print handouts in braille or in extra-large font size?

➢ **Filming** – will you be filming your presentation? If so, you need to acknowledge that fact to participants; either by them individually signing a release form or having a sign at the entrance to your meeting room like the one below:

> **FILMING IN PROGRESS.**
> *By entering this area I understand that I may appear on camera and use of my image or voice may be used for advertising and/or trade purposes.*

The cameras need to be positioned in locations where they will not be bumped or damaged by participants moving about the room, with clear sightlines to the front of the room. Also, cameras need to be elevated so people will not walk in front of them and ruin your image.

➤ **Language** – will there be participants who do not speak your native language? Will you need to employ the services of an interrupter? If that is the case, remember it takes twice as long to convey your message because you need to speak and then give the interrupter time to translate. You may need to increase your class length or cut some of your content. Regional accents, slang, and word definitions can change from one locale to another, so make sure you are prepared for those minor language issues as well.

➤ **Bathrooms** – people cannot concentrate with a full bladder. You need to build-in frequent bathroom breaks into your program, hopefully at the end of discussing a topic. Make break times seamless as if they flow with your topics. Rule of thumb for adults is every 60 – 90 minutes, offer a 10 - 15 minute break. Try not to go over two hours between breaks. You don't want people to miss any of your content because they excused themselves in the middle of your presentation, which is also very disruptive to the entire audience.

➤ **Unexpected** – there could be personal emergencies arise on behalf of a participant over which you have no control. Things like low blood sugar, stroke, heart attack, dropping dead, headache, food poisoning, slip and fall, laceration, or a multitude of other rare issues. The only way to prepare for something like these is to know how to rapidly contact emergency services for your location.

Being proactive instead of reactive on all these points listed above will ensure a smooth program. It's all dependent on your pre-planning! Try to visit the location several days ahead of time to assess any of these problems which may arise. Survey your participants to see if accommodations for handicap or language issues need to be handled. On the day of the event, arrive extra early to inspect the location: check temperature levels, test all audio and video equipment to make sure they are all in great working order. Bring extra *fresh* batteries with you for all electronic devices. And just in case there is a complete A/V failure, have all your notes printed in a three-ring binder as a back-up copy, so you can still proceed with your training.

Be Captivating!

Merriam-Webster dictionary defines captivating as, *"charmingly or irresistibly appealing,"* and that is who you need to be as a trainer. By fostering an appealing learning environment and subject matter for your participants, they will find you irresistible and charming! Here are eight points to help you be captivating; not only personally, but also in your content:

1. Be passionate – in all endeavors of your life. Let that passion be seen by others.

2. Show humility – be humble. Arrogance is a turn-off!

3. Have a sense of humor – learn to roll with the punches. Laugh and be fun to be around.

4. Be different – don't be like every other trainer. Be yourself and let a little quirkiness of yourself be known.

5. Show interest in others – not only in people but also in a wide range of topics. Be well-read and familiar with current topics.

6. Be curious – be open-minded with a healthy sense of curiosity.

7. Give more – always give a little more than what people are expecting.

8. Remove fears – make people feel comfortable around you. Help people remove their fears of learning and of your subject matter.

Supportive Research

A 2019 study at the University of Arizona concluded that learning is optimized when we fail 15% of the time. To learn new things, we must sometimes fail. If someone always passes with 100%, then they are not learning, and the content is too easy for them. This study looked at the right amount of failure to optimize learning and that ended up being a 15% failure or 85% success rate. Therefore, when designing your content, don't make it too easy. Design a class to make people think with a built-in 85% success rate.

The goal throughout this book is to give you tips and techniques to make you stand out and be different from every other mediocre trainer. This chapter is particularly important for you to create content with several of these learning theories in mind. Using a combination of these learning theories will put you on the path of a captivating trainer!

It's appropriate to close this chapter with a summation from Howard Gardner:

"Everyone has strengths and weaknesses in various intelligences, which is why educators should decide how best to present course material given the subject-matter and individual class of students. Indeed, instruction designed to help students learn material in multiple ways can trigger their confidence to develop areas in which they are not as strong. In the end, students' learning is enhanced when instruction includes a range of meaningful and appropriate methods, activities, and assessments."

Chapter 9

Presentation Modes

"I cannot teach anybody anything. I can only make them think." ~ Socrates

So far in this section of chapters, we have learned:

➢ How to conduct a needs analysis to determine what information needs to be taught and to whom.

➢ How to incorporate various learning theories into your presentations for optimum audience comprehension.

➢ Now, in this chapter you will learn ways to disseminate your message.

Your presentation methodology will be different if you are giving an informal versus formal presentation. An informal or casual presentation would be a planned or extemporaneous short talk given to your work team members, a business networking group, family, or friends, or anytime you are put on the spot to talk; typically to a group of people you know. A formal presentation would be one where you are made aware ahead of time and you prepare for the event; typically, in a more structured professional environment for a group of people you may or may not know. Formal presentations usually follow processes of instructional system design and use proper English and sentence structure, while informal may be a little more relaxed.

ISD – Instructional System Design ADDIE

Everyone in the training profession needs an awareness of the fundamentals of the standardized Instructional System Design (ISD) process known as *ADDIE*, **A**nalysis, **D**esign, **D**evelopment, **I**mplementation, and **E**valuation. This gold-standard for designing training programs is particularly important when you are developing a formal training process, especially one with multiple trainers or a train-the-trainer format. Also, it is doubly important to follow this format if your program is grant funded and you will need to report processes and analytics to funders; or if your program will offer professional CEU's.

The following five-step ADDIE model will help you organize your message goals into a flow which can be easily used by any trainer and with any verbal or technological presentation method.

1. <u>Analysis</u>

- Analyze the organization's goals, needs, jobs and tasks of the target audience, and the beneficial impact on the overall organization.

- This step identifies the training needs.

2. <u>Design</u>

- Identify the outcomes and strategies. Decide how to structure the sequence of your message points.

- Make sure your defined outcomes are aligned with the organization's strategies and needs.

3. **Development**

- Create various learning events and activities to support the organization's needs.

- Make sure these educational activities are aligned with the defined outcomes.

4. **Implementation**

- Develop your implementation plan as to presentation methods; along with when and where the course(s) will be offered.

- Physically deliver (transfer knowledge to students). It's best to test with a small pilot group before a complete roll-out.

5. **Evaluation**

- Assess effectiveness of training by making sure lessons learned have been incorporated into the organization's processes.

- Collect student and organization feedback.

How does the ISD model align with the chapters within this book?

➢ Analysis - Chapters 7 and 10

➢ Design - Chapters 8 and 11

➢ Development – Chapter 8

Is Technology Effective?

Email, voicemail, text messages, eFax, smart phones, iPads, emoji's, and laptop computers are all wonderful tools which help us communicate. These modern devices, along with those yet to be developed in the future, may increase our professional and personal efficiency, but very often, they decrease our effectiveness! When communication really counts, most people fall back on the original solution; that being face-to-face conversation. The presumption of this book is the most effective workplace training is still done on a personal level; that of face-to-face in either small groups or large audience settings. Thus, the reason we have spent so much time discussing the importance of topics like: body language, proxemics, and the ability to properly speak.

We all can relate to having text messages, emails, and even voicemails misinterpreted or taken out of context because there are no supporting modes of communication to properly express feelings and intent via those modern technological devices. In this chapter, we will continue with that presumption, but will also be expanding our view into additional technological methods of training that currently exist as of today.

Speaking Through Centuries

The spoken word goes back farther than recorded history, even if it was only *grunts*. The act of speaking or the profession of an *orator* has lasted for thousands of years and is still more effective than many advances in technology. Speech has survived: hieroglyphics, the chisel and rock, parchment paper and quill pen, chalk and slate, the typewriter, the printing press; and seems to still be more effective than many of today's modern computer applications. As humans evolved, so did communication styles.

Language is always evolving and so are the meanings and interpretations of both spoken and written words. Here is a good example:

> Older generations used the ellipsis (three dots) "..." as a way to indicate a continuation, loss of thought, or to create mystery. However, younger generations view the ellipsis as a passive-aggressive power play.

Therefore, the modes of how you present your materials need to consider all positive and negative aspects of communication interpretations. Your presentation methods will change based on the content to be presented, length of time you have to teach materials, and the composition and location of your audience, and a formal versus informal environment.

ILT – Instructor Led Training

Instructor led training can occur live, in-person, in a classroom type scenario or via an Internet video broadcast method. As this book was started to be written during a global pandemic, the rise of video broadcasting methods is soaring due to social distancing and the halt of large gatherings and international travel. New Internet broadcast platforms are emerging, trying to keep up with this unprecedented global demand. Trainers have to find a new norm and comfort level of speaking into a camera without the luxury of having their audience in the room with them to assess energy and body language cues. Whatever the new global normalcy will become, assuredly there will be a higher rate of future Internet based training than there was pre-pandemic.

There are four basic types of instructor-led training which we will review:

1. One to One – One to one training is where a trainer is instructing a single student. This is often seen in cases of private tutoring, mentoring, or coaching; with the student having 100% focus of the trainer. This is a rare exception in workplace training because it is so costly and time consuming to focus on each student individually. We see this type of training happening more often at upper management levels when an employee is promoted to take over for someone retiring or a shift in job duties.

2. One to Many – A one to many training environment is the majority of training scenarios. There are some benefits of having one trainer teach a room full or an online group of people. A trainer's time is leveraged more effectively by delivering the message to more people; and the trainer is perceived more of an expert and authority figure when speaking in front of a large group. There is a downfall to this scenario and that is, the larger the group, the higher the chance of having hecklers and people to disrupt your program.

3. Tag Team Training – Tag team training usually occurs in the one-to-many situations but may also be seen in a

one-on-one environment. Think of tag team training as running a relay race. Instead of handing off a baton to the next runner, you hand off content to your co-trainer. This format uses two or more trainers who may have a bit more expertise in different pieces of subject matter within the program. This format also works great for full-day or multi-day training events so each individual trainer can maintain their energy and vocal stamina. This training format is also engaging for the audience because each trainer has a different personality and teaching style, thus keeping your audience attentive.

4. Train the Trainer – This training format is a peer teaching scenario. Typically, a lead trainer is instructing a group of fellow trainers on the desired program. The audience members will then take the same content and instruct numerous groups. This allows for the content to be taught to a greater number of people in a shorter amount of time. Usually, the lead trainer is the one who wrote the original program, so the audience can ask detailed questions and expect precise answers from the expert. Consistency is paramount in these training situations because the original content must be exactly the same between whoever is teaching it! This is particularly important if there are CEUs awarded.

Educational Technologies

Technologies in training have progressed in the past few decades. At first, there were chalkboards and flipcharts; then progressed to the big technological advancement of an overhead projector which used transparencies (*Ok...I am this old!*). Then, the next greatest tool for trainers was the invention of computers with PowerPoint, especially the portability of a laptop and LCD projector.

PowerPoint is one of the only software products we will mention by name, because others are changing too often and may not be relevant when you are reading this book. PowerPoint was an amazing achievement because you could maintain consistency, especially in train the trainer scenarios. The file of slides could be distributed to other trainers, and everyone would have identical content. Also, by using the *notes feature*, instructor specific messages and reference materials could be listed. Another productive feature of PowerPoint, if you don't want to connect it to an LCD projector and display on a screen, is to use it on a laptop with the screen facing you and using it like a teleprompter for your notes.

Your best option is to do an Internet search for whatever specific piece of training/teaching software you are thinking of using. You will get a list of all current choices, and some resources also list reviews and comparisons of several options. The other must attend event is ATD's TechKnowledge Conference. ATD is the Association for Talent Development and was formerly known as ASTD American Society for Training and Development. This is a yearly conference highlighting all the advances in educational training technologies. There is more information on them in the *Reference Section* at the back of this book.

SPT – Self Paced Training

Self-paced training is individual learning; meaning you study when you want and at your own pace. This mode of training has exploded in popularity with the invention of so many Internet-based learning platforms.

However, before technology, students would learn on their own by purchasing a textbook and accompanying workbook; with and without the option for open-book exams to test their progress. This method of using study guides and workbooks can still be found in some situations today, but more companies are implementing online learning options as their pricing drops, availability increases, and they become easier to use.

Online or eLearning software systems, also called platforms, have expanded the education market around the world. Many colleges and universities can know attract students from anywhere for a lower tuition investment. Institutions like University of Phoenix and Southern New Hampshire University are cashing-in on online learning. Corporations saw the benefit of online training opportunities from the highly successful use in academia. The original eLearning platforms were very expensive and cumbersome to use – they took a dedicated IT staff to maintain. However, with advances in technology and an increase in demand, we now see inexpensive easy-to-use systems. So reasonable in fact, that small businesses, nonprofits, and even individual trainers and coaches can offer online courses.

Most eLearning companies offer free demos and trial periods for you to explore their products. Conduct your due diligence and research to find the best system that will work for your needs and within your budget.

Cellphones are now becoming a popular tool for online learning. Most eLearning software platforms are scaling their systems to work not only on a full-size computer screen, but also on a small smartphone screen. Everyone's smartphone has Internet access and can connect to eLearning online systems, where some people may not have easy access to a computer or Internet connectivity from a computer.

The increased use of cellphones in training has seen an increase in negative outcomes:

> Cellphones, with a smaller screen, are harder to use; especially if having to type longer responses. Headaches and eye fatigue are greater due to smaller screens.

> Too much of a casual approach to learning? People can pick up the lesson on their phone when sitting in a parking lot, watching TV, or being distracted by a multitude of other inputs. The sense of importance to the content is decreased if students don't value materials accessed from a casual setting.

> A decrease in retention of the concepts has been seen. Maybe because people get distracted with calls and text messages on the same device, and are not paying full attention and concentrating on learning the materials.

Older students will have difficulty taking an online class via a cellphone, which is another factor to consider if implementing self-paced training options.

VR - Virtual Reality

Virtual reality came into prominence in entertainment via video games, and has gained widespread appeal in medical and military training. VR is a simulated experience which may or may not duplicate real-world environments. This is why it's so popular in medical and military training applications. Students can practice surgeries and military combat operations repeatedly to gain precision in a low-cost, low-risk environment. VR is also the basis for flight simulators when training pilots.

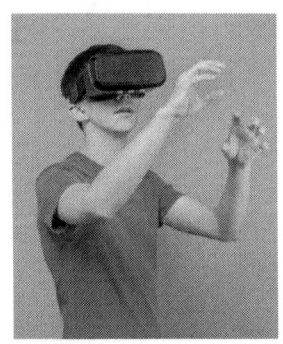

When using immersive VR techniques, a person wears a headset which changes their view as they move their head. It immerses them into a three-dimensional reality; using realistic images, sounds, and other sensations which stimulates a user's physical presence in this virtual environment as if they truly were there. Some large corporations and military operations are designing VR rooms which use specially designed large screens on the walls, ceiling, and floors to project the virtual images for a whole-body interactive experience instead of just the headsets.

A 2019 research study at the University of Nottingham in England concluded:

A new study suggests employee safety could be improved through the use of virtual reality (VR) in Health and Safety training, such as fire evacuation drills. Researchers developed an immersive VR system to stimulate participant's perception of temperature, and senses of smell, sight, and hearing to explore how they behaved during health and safety training scenarios. Previous research on human behavior during real-world fire incidents showed a lack of understanding of fire spread and movement, which meant occupants were unprepared and would misjudge appropriate evacuation actions. VR safety training enables employers to train staff on hazards and hazardous environments without putting anyone at risk. Therefore, they would be prepared for a real-world event and would save lives.

A study in 2018 at the University of Maryland found:

An 8.8 percent overall improvement in the recall accuracy using VR headsets, which is a statistically substantial number according to the research team.

As VR technology is becoming more widespread with lower investment costs to implement, we might start seeing an increase in training applications. Currently, the area of workplace training which embraces VR faster than other areas is that of occupational safety. Hazardous situations can be simulated via VR and students can learn how to spot dangerous situations and steps needed to mitigate the danger. The use of VR in workplace training is waiting for new creative training professionals like you, to incorporate it into other aspects of a workplace environment.

Gamification

The use of games for learning is nothing new; they have been around for decades. Companies can even buy customized versions of *Monopoly* for teaching their business concepts. The U.S. Department of Defense has been using video games for years to simulate disaster scenarios with soldiers, sailors, Marines, and local emergency departments. A 2010 research study at the University of Colorado-Denver summarized:

> They discovered those using video games had an 11 percent higher factual knowledge level, a 14 percent higher skill-based knowledge level, and a 9 percent higher retention rate than trainees in comparison groups who did not learn the same content via video game applications.

However, the word *Gamification* seems to be a new buzzword thrown around by workplace trainers. Gamification is a newer concept having its roots in the video game industry. Wikipedia defines *Gamification*, "The gamification of learning is an educational approach to motivate students to learn by using video game design and game elements in learning environments. The goal is to maximize enjoyment and engagement through capturing the interest of learners and inspiring them to continue learning."

Some believe that gamifying your training has positive points like:

➢ It's fun and engaging.

➢ It's easier for learners to retain knowledge.

➢ Creates recognition by rewarding learners with actual prizes or certificates. Like getting a gold star when you were in Kindergarten.

➢ Drives behavioral change.

Others believe that gamifying your training has negative outcome like:

➢ It is only a short-term fix to longer-term on-going problems.

➢ Addresses symptoms within an organization, but doesn't fix any of the underlying issues.

➢ Gamification is disrespectful to employees because it trivializes them. Like getting a gold star for accomplishment.

Gallup did a poll and found that 70% of employees are disengaged, which supports the comment by the late comedian George Carlin:

"Most people work just hard enough not to get fired and get paid just enough money not to quit!"

That research poll is why some say gamification may be the correct training methodology to boost employee engagement. If we have seen anything come out of the video game industry, it is the addictive nature and long-term focused engagement a player exhibits when immersed in that type of escapist fantasy world. Which are good qualities workplace trainers are trying to implement in workplace scenarios via gamification. If employees would put as much effort into their workplace tasks as they do when they are at home playing a video game, industries would see a huge increase in productivity. There are hundreds of online articles on how to implement gamification strategies into your organization. There are also several software applications which take your content and gamify it. You are best to do online research for the most current updated list of vendors because the principles of this training mode are rapidly changing with technological advancements.

Hybrid / Blended Learning

Blended learning is an approach to education which combines online educational modes with traditional in-person classroom methods. It requires the physical presence of both trainer and student for the classroom component, with some elements of student control over time, place, path, or pace via the online component.

There are pros and cons to 100% online or 100% in-person training modes. In-person training can be costly and disruptive to an organization if an entire staff has to go to a remote location for training. However, there are many positives coming from personal interactions and the open sharing of ideas, while being able to implement several different learning strategies from the previous chapter.

Programs that constitute 100% online content may be restrictive to older generations who typically are not as computer literate, and the ability to interact with other students or sometimes even ask questions for clarification are not present in some online platforms.

As we have said many times in this book, your optimum choice will be dependent on the composition of your audience and the content of your program. But, blended or hybrid learning may be the best option if you can incorporate the best of the components from online and classroom learning modes.

Difficult Behaviors

Graduating to the level of a professional workplace trainer is when you can successfully combat hecklers in your audience! Inevitably, you will be blessed with those participants who make it their mission to grandstand and let people see how great they think they are. These people are present in both in-person and online training events; and you don't always have the luxury to just hit a *mute* button. This is one reason you should study stand-up comics to see how they deal with hecklers.

> **"Your behavior's so loud; I can't hear what you're saying!"** Is a play on Ralph Waldo Emerson's quote, **"Who you are speaks so loudly; I can't hear what you're saying!"**

In his book *Coping With Difficult People*, Dr. Robert Bramson exposes the seven behavior patterns which are the most disruptive and frustrating for a trainer to endure:

1. **Hostile-Aggressives** – These people try to overwhelm or *bully* by bombarding others, making snide remarks, or throwing tantrums when things don't go their way. There are three types of behaviors most often seen with this group:

   a. *Sherman Tank* – come on charging, open attacks

   b. *Sniper* – take pot shots; launch verbal missiles

   c. *Exploder* – sudden responses; fearsome attacks

2. **Complete Complainers** – These people gripe incessantly but never try to do anything about what they complain about, either because they feel powerless

to do so, or because they refuse to bear any responsibility.

    a. *Whiners* – monotonous and screechy voice

    b. *Triangular Complainer* – complain to you, not at you

3. **Silent and Unresponsive** – These are the people who respond to every question or suggestion with: *yep, no,* or a *grunt*. They act like a *clam* and just close down.

4. **Super-Agreeables** – These people appear agreeable and sincere, some almost obedient, but then don't produce what they say they will or then act contrary to the way they have led you to expect.

5. **Negativists** – These are the vocal objectors, "It won't work!" or "It's impossible!" They defeat any optimism from the rest of the group.

    a. *Wet Blanket* – "…just won't work."

    b. *Yes But-ter* – "…yes, but…"

6. **Know-It-All Experts** – These are those superior people who believe, and want you to recognize that they (think they) know everything there is to know about anything and everything worth knowing! They're condescending, imposing, and pompous; while trying to make you feel like an idiot.

    a. *Bulldozers* – push their ideas and opinions

    b. *Balloons* – phony 'know-it-all' exert; BS'er

7. **Indecisives** – Those people who stall major decisions until the decision is made for them, those who can't let go of anything until it is perfect.

   a. *Stallers* – maybe; we'll see; I'm not sure; evading

You will become a more polished professional when you have *come backs* to combat disruptive behaviors. A great one is to stand next to the heckler while continuing to speak; it makes them feel intimidated!

Final Thoughts

In a world where technology is quickly taking over, it is important that younger generations understand that older generations are willing to adapt to technology. But conversely, the younger generations have to realize that there is value in face-to-face communication and must set aside technological devices and learn to become more *personable!* People value time differently and your choice of the presentation mode must take that key factor into account when designing your training programs. Blending multiple learning strategies from the previous chapter with multiple presentation modes from this chapter will guarantee you positively impact more people.

Share your expectations with all involved! Regardless of age or generational labels, no one wants to operate in a workplace based on a set of assumptions. Clarity of purpose and goals for each of your training programs will ensure your success.

> **"Success without purpose is a pretty meaningless life."**
> ~ Zac Efron

Chapter 10

Socratic Method

> *"True wisdom comes to each of us when we realize how little we understand about life, ourselves, and the world around us."* ~ Socrates

There is an ancient and interesting teaching method which has eluded many a trainer's prior education, including mine. For me, I went through high school in the late 1970's and college in the 1980's; but I do not remember at all ever being introduced to the Socratic Method of teaching. Maybe it's because I went to public school and not some hoity-toity private institution, but let's review this methodology and see how, if, and where, it could be incorporated into workplace training.

The Socratic Method is a bit esoteric and hard to put into a definitive structure, which then, also limits the scope of its applications. It is based on ancient Greek philosophies of Socrates. It places the teacher or trainer into a more submissive role, denying their own knowledge of the topic, while allowing students to foster an open dialogue with each other on the topic. It supposedly allows the students to draw their own conclusions on the subject. This is designed for small-group discussions, where the group is sitting in a circle facing each other to encourage greater dialogue. The rest of the classroom sits in a larger circle around the smaller one, while observing the smaller group's dialogue. Think of the ancient Colosseum in Rome or the Acropolis in Greece, with a small group of debaters on the main floor and the greater audience sitting in the seats observing.

Just because a group of people are facing each other and engaged in open dialogue, does that guarantee they will make factual or pertinent conclusions? Or does this foster individuals vying to substantiate their own beliefs or prejudices in the group as it pertains to the topic? The teacher/trainer is in a moderator role to make sure creative questions are used within the group to dissect and ignore current thoughts on the topic; while the group is to form or propose new thoughts on the topic. Because of this dynamic, Socratic Method teaching manuals warn about using this method in scientific or mathematic settings, or anywhere there is a definitive answer. It is suggested for more subjective discipline discussions like: philosophy, humanities, art, ethics, and even religion. However, I wasn't even introduced to this methodology while going through Seminary.

While doing some research for a Human Resource project, I came across the Socratic Method on a job posting for a teaching position within a Medical Assistant school. I was a bit flabbergasted by seeing a medical related school saying on a job posting, that a requirement for this teaching position is having practical knowledge of the Socratic Method. My question was, "Why?" Do you, as a patient, really want a lower-level medical assistant to engage you in a discussion on the merits of why your severed bleeding finger is not a good thing to have happen to you? Or do you want them to jump into action from their practical medical training and suture your finger?

Now, I will admit that the Socratic Method of discussion may be useful if a group of cancer doctors are consulting on the best course of action for a patient with a rare type of cancer; but from all I know, those types of discussions are not needed, nor should be encouraged at a medical assistant level of training. Do you think the HR professional who wrote that job posting really knew what they were talking about when listing Socratic Method on the job posting? Or do you think it is like listing Adult Training Theories on postings; just throwing around big words and phrases when they really don't understand the underlying applications?

So, why did I separate this discussion on the Socratic Method into its own small chapter? Many educators espouse the Socratic technique as a teaching modality which should have been discussed in Chapter 8 on Delivery Methods. Others might say since it is a small-group interactive dynamic, then maybe it should be discussed as a Presentation Mode in Chapter 9. However, based on my research and opinion, it has better applications, as pertaining to workplace training, as a Needs Analysis tool and would fit best in Chapter 7. If engaging smaller group discussions to actively dissect and ignore current thoughts on the topic, and proposing new thoughts, while the facilitator takes a submissive/subservient role; isn't that the best scenario for an effective Needs Analysis outcome?

Since the Socratic Process works best on esoteric, philosophical, or objective type discussions, questions like these below seem most beneficial:

➢ "What is beauty?"

> "What is life?"

> "Who or what is God?"

> "How do you value humanity?"

What types of questions could we use in a small-group, circular discussion format to benefit training in the workplace?

> "How could we improve workplace performance?"

> "What motivates volunteers to give of themselves?"

> "What self-motivates an employee?"

> "How can we increase adherence to safety guidelines?"

> "What additional training opportunities should we offer? And why?"

The method is a collective inquiry between the participants of the small group. There is no one single right answer, just many perspectives. The open exchange of ideas is geared to collectively make meaning. The participants seek and gain a deeper understanding of the topic through thoughtful dialogue rather than rote memorization. Since the facilitator is not encouraging a single correct answer, individual participants gain a greater sense of value for their active dialogue. In summary, a little more hard-core definition is:

The Socratic Method searches for general commonly held truths that shape beliefs and scrutinizes them to determine their consistency with other beliefs. The basic form is a series of questions formulated as tests of logic and fact intended to help a person or group discover their beliefs about some topic, explore definitions, and characterize universal characteristics shared by various particular instances.

Workplace Preparation

A trainer has to know ahead of time if they are going to engage in Socratic Methods.

✓ The room has to be arranged in a circle or oval with everyone facing each other, or several small-group circles.

✓ Questions need to be prepared ahead of time. These questions need to focus on the ideas, philosophies, and moral dilemmas pertaining to the topic.

✓ Questions should not review or encourage facts.

✓ A secure environment where participants know they are respected and won't be criticized for their open beliefs.

✓ The role of the trainer/facilitator is to make sure everyone is actively engaging.

✓ The facilitator must keep the discussion moving forward with additional clarification questions once a participant makes a statement. Clarification questions such as:

  ➢ "How did you come to that conclusion?"

  ➢ "Do you think we can adopt that principle company-wide?"

> ➤ "Do you think we will see any negative repercussions to adopting that principle? If so, what are some options to mitigate them?"

Do you agree this could be a more useful methodology in a Needs Analysis project? How and where could you implement this methodology dedicated back to the ancient Greek philosopher Socrates?

Chapter 11

Assessment

> **"When the cook tastes the soup, that's formative assessment. When the customer tastes the soup, that's summative assessment"** ~ Paul Black

Analytics and assessment are the final critical components to a successful training operation. Assessment goals are usually threefold:

1. How pertinent was the material to each employee?

2. Did the presented content align with the objectives of the program?

3. How effective was the trainer at presenting the content for optimum comprehension?

There must be congruency between your needs analysis, content, and analytics. Your needs analysis process will uncover what you need to teach, you better teach that content, and finally you will be judged on how well you taught it. You can't go through a needs analysis process and find a gap in knowledge about oranges, develop content all about oranges; but then conduct post-training assessments by asking the participants how they liked apples!

A post-training assessment is how a company, or your boss, will judge you on your effectiveness as a trainer. This will determine whether you are fired, deserve a pay raise; or in the case of a contract trainer, whether you will be re-hired on another project. It is always advantageous for you to have a role in developing the assessment component, to make sure the process and questions will show you in the best possible light. Throughout this chapter we will look at a few techniques to help develop fair and honest assessment tools, while still having a slight advantage in your favor.

You can offer post-course surveys or questionnaires either in a paper format, having them complete the forms before leaving your class, or online software options. Searching for current online systems will give you many options, some free and some fee based. Research what would work best for your needs and budget.

Train To Your Audience

Your assessment will be determined on how well you connected with the participants, not only with the content, but also with your personality. Your program has to be pertinent and understandable by your participants.

If you are a PhD scientist training other doctorate educated professionals, then speak at their level. However, if you are training the mainstream employee, remember the average adult comprehension and reading level in the USA is that of an 8th grader. You might need to 'dummy-down' your presentation and vocabulary to match the level of your audience. If not, you will fail assessments because they will not understand what you are trying to teach them.

Being a workplace trainer already makes you smarter than an 8th grader; due to your awareness of multiple topics, ability to speak in front of a group, and your capacity to dissect the *big picture* into its component pieces. Just don't be intimidating while training! Be relatable!

Structuring Assessment Questions

As you are developing the assessment component of each training program, it's necessary to plan questions according to these criteria:

➢ Make every question count. Make sure each question you ask adds value and drives response data that relates directly to your training goals. If it's not pertinent, don't ask it.

➢ KISS = Keep it short and simple. Respondents are less likely to complete long surveys, or surveys which bounce around haphazardly from one topic to another.

➢ Ask direct questions. Questions should focus on a specific situation or behavior rather than a general tendency. This urges respondents to stick to facts rather than abstract ideas, emotions, or beliefs.

➢ Ask one question at a time. Do not double up on questions. If you have an 'and' in your question, think about breaking it up into two separate questions.

➢ Start with straightforward questions. Ease your respondent into the survey by asking easy questions at the beginning of your questionnaire, then move into more complex or thought-provoking elements once you already have them engaged in the process.

➢ Rephrase yes/no questions. Yes/no questions provide less detailed and usable response data. Think about rephrasing from yes/no to "How much," "How often," or "How likely" questions.

➢ Avoid leading and biased questions. Certain words and phrases can introduce bias into your questions or point the respondent in the direction of a particular answer. Try to keep your point of view out of questions. Double-check your use of adjectives and adverbs in your questions. If they are not needed, remove them. Ask open-ended questions instead of leading questions. A leading question example would be, "Do you see how implementing X would decrease time spent on the task?" Rephrasing that to remove bias would be, "What do you see as a benefit of implementing X?"

Tasks vs Philosophy

In Chapter 8 we discussed the differences between adult and child learners, and workplace and academic training. Since adult workplace training is more task oriented instead of philosophical like academic teaching, your assessment questions need to address the task aspects of what you taught. Try to stay away from *touchy-feely* questions because they are hard to evaluate, and they depend so much on individual biases, subjective opinions, and participant emotions. Ask assessment questions like:

1. How was the course practical?

2. How was the training relevant to your needs?

3. How did the training content meet your expectations?

4. Do you have any suggestions to improve this course?

5. What are two items you can immediately implement into your workplace routine starting tomorrow morning?

"Some training courses depend too much on cognitive learning, using only lectures and slide presentations. This type of learning requires the learner to passively absorb and retain large amounts of content. To retain learning, learners need opportunities to make a connection with the content and apply the learning to real-life."
~ Robert F. Mager

Trainer Assessment

Here are a few questions to rate your performance as an instructor:

1. How would you rate the quality of the instructor?

2. What was the instructor's level of content knowledge?

3. How would you rate their organization and preparation?

4. How was their enthusiasm?

Types of Assessment

Formative and summative are two important types of educational assessment:

- Formative is assessment **for** learning. This is an ongoing assessment which allows teachers to monitor students on a day-to-day basis. Teachers can modify their teaching based on what students need to be successful. Formative provides students with timely and specific feedback needed to make adjustments in their learning or implementation of the topics. This would be equivalent to a mentoring program within the workplace.

- Summative is assessment **of** learning. This is a snapshot in time and lets the teacher, and students, know how well a student has done at completing learning tasks and activities. Summative provides information about achievement, useful reporting information; but has little to no effect on learning. In an academic setting, it would equate to a midterm or a final exam. In workplace training, this equates to post-training assessments and surveys which we are discussing in this chapter.

Here are a couple examples of each type of assessment:

➢ Formative = in-class discussions, group discussions, weekly quizzes, hypothetical questions.

➢ Summative = instructor-created exams, final projects, final essays, standardized tests.

Depending on the type of information you need to teach, and to whom, it might be beneficial to offer a post-course mentoring component to increase the formative assessment.

Below are a few other standardized types of educational assessment:

✓ Diagnostic Assessment – Before creating content, get to know the student's strengths, weaknesses, skills, and their baseline knowledge. This may be conducted as part of a Needs Analysis process as discussed in Chapter 7.

✓ Confirmative Assessment – A confirming process to see if the content you historically have been teaching is still pertinent and appropriate.

✓ Norm-Referenced Assessment – This compares a student's performance against the average norm. Another example would be when a teacher compares the average grade of their students against the average grade of the entire school. A workplace could compare test scores against nationwide averages.

✓ Criterion-Reference Assessment – It measures a student's performance against a fixed set of criteria or learning standards. This is used to evaluate a specific body of knowledge or skill set. It's a test to evaluate the curriculum taught in a course. A workplace would use criteria set forth by an accrediting or government agency.

✓ Ipsative Assessment – This compares a student's performance against themselves. A person uses this method to improve themselves by comparing previous results. A workplace example of this would be offering a pre-test and then a post-test so see the improvement of knowledge.

Common Sense

Unfortunately, you cannot teach common sense, street smarts, or critical thinking. A high degree of your follow-up assessment will be based on how well your course participants have mastered these innate qualities. *Street smarts* is that shrewd awareness of how to survive or succeed in any situation. We all know highly educated and degreed people so versed in book knowledge, but stupid in *common-sense* everyday living situations.

Critical thinking is the next level. It is the ability to think clearly and rationally, understanding the logical connection between ideas. It is the ability to engage in reflective and independent thinking. You will find older generations typically having a greater ability at critical thinking skills. People with critical thinking skills can:

- Understand the links between ideas.

- Comprehend the importance and relevance of arguments, discussions, and ideas.

- Identify inconsistencies and errors in reasoning.

- Approach problems in a consistent and systematic way.

People having these qualities will be your best students, hold you to task, but appreciate you as a trainer. Each of you reading this book must already be experts in critical thinking, because these are skills most crucial for being an effective trainer.

Your assessment scores will be based on how well you can present your content in small pieces and link the material to direct applications for each trainee. Remember, most people don't have the comprehension to see or do it themselves – so you have to make it blatantly obvious to them! Training the obvious will gain you higher grades as a trainer.

Research Conclusion

A 2012 research study published by the *Association for Psychological Science* looked at the science of training and development within organizations. They wanted to pinpoint what really matters and what really works. In 2012, in the United States, employers spent $135 billion training their employees, but employers knew those billions of dollars do not always improve the workplace because the skills taught do not transfer to the actual job.

The greatest discovery was business leaders and management need to view training as a universal system and not just a one-time event. Meaning, what happens before and after the actual training is equally as important as the training itself. These following three points will increase effectiveness:

1. Training is more effective when various jobs within an organization have been analyzed, the skill set of its employees are understood, supervisors and

leaders are all on the same page, and trainees are motivated to learn. (Needs Analysis).

2. During the training, sufficient structure and guidance should be offered to trainees while still giving them opportunities to make decisions about their learning experience. (Adult/Montessori learning principles).

3. After the training, trainees should have ample time and opportunities to use what they have learned in the real world with real feedback. (Formative/Mentoring).

Before an organization implements a training program, staff and management need to plan-out the following:

✓ What training strategy will be employed?

✓ What steps will be taken to ensure trainees are adequately engaged, motivated, and challenged?

✓ What will the organization do before and after the training to ensure trainees can and will use what they have learned?

Final Thought

It is comforting to see the contents and structure of this book are supported by scientific research studies. Nothing should stop you on your great adventure of being an effective professional workplace trainer!

> **"What's the worst type of presentation? One with too much information! What's the best type of presentation? One that moves people!"** ~Ideou.com

Section IV: Resources

Chapter 12

Ice Breakers

Ice breakers are a very important component at the beginning of your speaking or training program. They are designed to engage the audience and make them feel relaxed, safe, and open-minded; it gets them ready to hear what you are going to say.

Most trainers do not consider their introduction as an ice breaker; but in actuality, it is the most important way to set the tone for your program. It puts your audience at ease by letting them know why you are in front of them and your qualifications for training on the subject matter. You really cannot step in front of a group and start reading your list of accomplishments and expertise as to why you are there; that would sound too egotistical. Therefore, it is important to have someone else introduce you. But you *NEVER* allow someone to go out and 'wing-it' with your introduction. You must write your own introduction ahead of time and hand it to someone else to read as you are welcomed in front of the room. Another trick of professionals is to have your standard introduction printed and laminated so whoever reads it is not shuffling paper;

being laminated, you are sure to get it back to use at your next event.

What can you do if there is no one to introduce you? A cool trick is to have your introduction professionally recorded by a voice-over artist, preferably someone of the opposite sex as you; this will remove any confusion as to your audience thinking it's you reading it. When you receive the digital audio file back from the recording studio, you will be able to embed the MP3 into a PowerPoint slide and play it before entering the room, or play it from your cell phone backstage before entering the room. This gives you the same effect as being introduced by a host or emcee without sounding boastful from doing it yourself.

Time and Size

The length of time you will be spending in front of the audience and the number of people in the audience will determine your introduction and the type of additional ice breakers you incorporate into your program. If it is a large group with an abbreviated time limit, then typically your introduction will be all you can do. If it is a small to mid-size group and you will be with them for several hours, then you can employ one of the following ice breakers after your introduction. If you will be with your audience for the entire day, then you might consider doing a second ice breaker when you return from lunch break. If you are with the same group for several days, then consider doing a different ice breaker each morning before you launch into your program.

Quote

Opening your program with an appropriate quote is an option for any size group. Make sure the quote ties in with the goals of your content and is by someone recognizable.

Audience Introductions

Go around the room one-by-one and have everyone introduce themselves with their name, their company (or department if all from same company), and one goal they want to take home from this program. This has to be brief and quick.

This is a fantastic way for you to make sure your content is in line with the expectations of the audience; if not, you can shift your content on the spot to make sure you address the concerns of the audience. A satisfied audience will give you higher scores on your assessment report.

Audience Strange Introductions

Have everyone, one-by-one, introduce themselves as a strange item, and why:

✓ A supermarket item

✓ A hardware store item

✓ An animal in the zoo

"Hi, my name is Sue and I'm a kangaroo because . . ."

Porn Name Introductions

Your porn name is derived from your first pet's name as your first name and your last name is the first street you grew up on. Have everyone introduce themselves this way. "Hi, I'm Fluffy Paradise!"

Fictitious Neighbor

Introduce the person sitting next to you and describe their fictitious life. The most creative and fun one will win X (X can be a copy of your book or a give-away item supplied by the trainer or company). "Hi everyone, sitting next to me is the amazing Burt. On the weekends he turns into a superhero and his power is …"

Question Introductions

You, as the trainer, facilitate these introductions by asking each person their name and one of the following questions. You can ask everyone the same question, or you can mix them up:

✓ What is your proudest accomplishment?

✓ What is the happiest moment in your life? Why?

✓ What is the scariest thing you have ever done for fun?

✓ What superpower do you want? Why?

✓ Where is one place you would love to travel to?

✓ What is something you were known for in high school?

✓ What was your favorite TV show as a kid?

✓ What song best describes you?

✓ Where was the most meaningful vacation you took?

✓ What is your favorite movie?

✓ Do you collect anything?

✓ What's a skill you learned when you were young that you still use today?

✓ What's the most valuable piece of career advice you've been given?

Gilligan Introduction

Have each person tell their name and describe three items they would want with them if stranded on an island, and why. You could preface this by saying, "Already on the island is: fresh cool drinking water, unlimited coconuts, and friendly lemurs." (Or whatever items you, as the trainer, make-up).

Check Sheet or Bingo Card

You prepare a sheet of paper or bingo-type card with any of the following. You give everyone 10-15 minutes to mingle and find someone in the audience who knows the answers to these questions. You could offer a prize for the person who found the most answers:

✓ Have two friends of another race

✓ Has been on a cruise

✓ Thoroughly understands another religion

✓ Owns a boat

✓ Knows someone in an interracial marriage

- ✓ Regularly eats at an ethnic restaurant

- ✓ Is a good cook

- ✓ Has experienced some type of prejudice

- ✓ Enjoys cleaning

- ✓ Knows the meaning behind Kwanzaa

- ✓ Knows the meaning behind Ramadan

- ✓ Knows the month Yom Kippur is celebrated

- ✓ Has traveled to Europe

- ✓ Nationality where Kim is popular last name

- ✓ Has children

- ✓ Has grandchildren

- ✓ Regularly attends ethnic festivals

- ✓ Has a boss with less formal education than you

- ✓ Nationality that will not put change in your hand

- ✓ Knows color and meaning of African unity flag

- ✓ Knows the colors of the gay pride flag

- ✓ Knows who celebrates Diwali

- ✓ Has a boss younger than you

- ✓ Knows meaning behind Cinco de Mayo

- ✓ Has worked with a person with a major disability

- ✓ Knows what The Balm in Gilead is

✓ Knows what year this is in the Chinese calendar

These questions above represent cultural diversity and acceptance. You can always design other questions relevant to your content or industry; even something like an OSHA safety bingo card or IT terminology sheet. Your creativity is endless.

Personality Assessment Fun Quiz*

*Due to the answers of number 3 and 4, this fun assessment should be done with care and with the proper audience who will enjoy the humor in it and not see it as a HR complaint!

Please read each of the four questions to your audience and give them time to write down their response. The analysis of each question is below. Read the analysis of each question and have a discussion as to their feelings on its accuracy. This is fun and has been amazingly accurate.

1. Name an animal and list 3 adjectives to describe that animal.

2. What is your favorite color and list 3 adjectives to describe the feeling that color gives you?

3. Name your favorite body of water (ex: a certain lake, river, ocean, sea, etc.) and list 3 adjectives that the feeling from that body of water gives you.

4. See yourself in a white room with no windows or doors. List 3 adjectives of how you feel in that setting.

Fun Quiz Analysis

1. These adjectives listed for question #1 are how your friends see you.

2. These adjectives listed for question #2 are how you see yourself.

3. These adjectives listed for question #3 are your feelings about sex.

4. These adjectives listed for question #4 are your thoughts on death/dying.

Take a Step

This ice breaker exercise can only be done in a large open room or outside. Everyone lines up along one wall, while facing the opposite wall. You have them take a step forward or backwards depending on the questions you ask. This example was designed for a healthcare conference:

✓ Take 1 step forward if you have enough money to meet your basic needs.

✓ Take 1 step forward if your race does not put you at risk of discrimination.

✓ Take 1 step forward if your sex does not put you at risk of discrimination.

✓ Take 1 step forward if your sexual orientation does not put you at risk of discrimination.

✓ Take 1 step forward if your age does not put you at risk of discrimination.

✓ Take 1 step forward if you are close to your family.

✓ Take 1 step forward if you have a secure and supportive network of friends around you.

✓ Take 1 step forward if you have a healthy lifestyle.

✓ Take 1 step backwards if you do not have good health insurance.

✓ Take 1 step backwards if your lifestyle behaviors put you at risk for heart disease.

This is a powerful visual representation of your group's dynamics based on the questions you ask. Hopefully, you can use this example as a foundation to re-write your own *Take a Step* based on your subject matter.

How Do Others See You?

[Requires pens, card stock, binder clips]

This ice breaker is only to be used in a group where all the participants know each other, as in being co-workers. Have everyone attach a sheet of heavy card stock paper on the backs of one another. It has to be cardstock, so it won't tear and end up writing on their shirts. Attach the sheets using a binder clip so it stays secure.

Instruct everyone to go to one another and write on their back **what you as a (friend/co-worker) see about this person**. This will be anonymous because you won't be able to see who is writing what (why we suggest you give everyone the same color pen to assure anonymity)! This ends up being a pretty truthful exercise, so you as the trainer need to be prepared for all reactions.

Chapter 13

Assessing Your Group

"We learn to do something by doing it. There is no other way." ~ John Holt

The following eight questions are those you should ask every person who books you to teach one of your programs. They will give you the background information needed to tailor your presentation to the audience's needs.

[topic] is replaced to represent your specific topic or subject matter for this group.

1. Who is my audience (employees, customers, general public, students, parents, inmates, etc.)?

2. What is the estimated size of the group?

3. Do the members of the group (audience) already know each other? In what context?

4. Why have I/we been asked to give this training?

5. How much is the group likely to know about [topic] and where have they acquired this information?

6. Does this group have any special characteristics or requirements about which I should know? Are there any areas of this topic I cannot discuss?

7. How is this group likely to feel about my topic? How might the special characteristics listed in question 6, such as values, education, or age affect their perception?

8. Is there anything I can do to make my message and presentation more appropriate to this audience? Anything that will make them more receptive to what I have to say?

You might have additional questions to add to this list, but this gives you a good foundation. These questions should be a standard form that you ask everyone who books you as a trainer.

Chapter 14

20 Persuasion Action Tips

The More You Apply, The More You'll Win

These following tips coupled with everything else you have learned in this book will help you win over your audience. Try to incorporate as many of these as you can when working with people. Some of these tips might be incorporated into your personal marketing materials, while others will be embedded into your training materials. Much success on your journey as a professional trainer!

1. Happy or Satisfied?

Do you want satisfied clients or happy clients? Are there customer satisfaction surveys or happiness surveys? Contrary to popular business culture, the correct answer is *happy clients*! Averages show that a happy client will tell 1 or 2 other people about your great service, while NOT happy clients tell 11 to 15 people about your bad service. Deeper emotions and feelings are attached to happiness. It is much harder to link any solid feelings to satisfaction levels. Since humans are emotional beings, the best speaking and sales professionals know how to frame positive emotions like that of happiness.

2. Pain or Pleasure

When framing your training presentations, refer to pain and pleasure hot topics with your audience. People will avoid pain more than they will move toward pleasure. In fact, studies show it is about a 2½ to 1 ration of movement from pain toward pleasure. Negative emotions are much stronger than positive emotions. Your job is to find your client's pain points during your needs analysis phase and embed those negative points into your presentation so they will better accept your positive training lessons.

3. Negative Framing

Never combine *you* and a negative into the same sentence. Make every association with you a positive one. For example: never say, "I won't take advantage of you." Say, "I will give you my best advice." Always be positive!

4. Have Them Take Notes

Research has shown that a person will rate or accept your content seven times more positively if they partake in an activity. Having your audience write on an outline or fill-in a worksheet during your presentation equates to an active participant in your program. Supplying a pen and worksheet about your presentation is critical to the positive comprehension and outcome of your training program.

5. Don't Be Arrogant

It's OK to play dumb and not know everything. Don't be a know-it-all; that just shows ignorance and arrogance on your part. It is perfectly OK to say, "I don't know that answer, but I will find out for you." But, then you must follow through and let them know what you found. If the audience thinks you are lying or making-up something just so you look good, then they will disregard your entire presentation.

6. Share Yourself

People will not trust you if you don't self-disclose. Share yourself with your audience. The best way to do that is through a short personal story that somehow ties in with the content of your presentation. But just like above, it must be a true personal story, not something made-up to fit the situation.

> **"They don't care about how much you know until they know how much you care."** ~ Zig Ziglar

7. Show Respect

You show respect by paying a sincere compliment to your audience, or at least a few people in the audience. Never use flattering compliments on their looks or clothing; make it more meaningful and appropriate to the situation. Statements like: "That was an astute observation," or "Really good comment," are fitting for any type of gathering.

Research conducted in November 2012 by Professor Sadato at the National Institute for Physiological Sciences in Japan showed, "To the brain, receiving a compliment is as much a social reward as being rewarded money. We've been able to find scientific proof that a person performs better when they receive a social reward after completing an exercise. There seems to be scientific validity behind the message, "praise to encourage improvement." Complimenting someone could become an easy and effective strategy to use in the classroom."

8. Commonness

Common bonds build an instant connection with people. Those bonds could be having the same friends, from the same area, same hobbies, liking the same foods, graduated from the same school, etc. However, a more powerful tool is having common enemies! Having a common enemy will bring your audience closer to you and your way of thinking; it makes them think that you are on their side. Common enemies could be: IRS, regulatory agencies, a certain competitor, etc. You must make sure that these common bonds or enemy has a direct correlation back to the content of your presentation or is pertinent to the market segment which you are speaking.

9. Trust

Trust is more powerful than truth. Unfortunately, we see how powerful this statement is with recent political characters. Knowing the people to whom you are speaking, and their belief structures builds trust. Trust will open many doors for you.

10. Be Precise

Precision, not generalities garners respect and acceptance. Remember the TV commercials about Ivory Soap being 99.44 % pure? A June 2013 research study at Columbia Business School showed, "people using precise dollar amounts were perceived to be more informed about the true value of the offer being negotiated." Precision shows your audience that you know what you are talking about and that you didn't grab some random number to make a point. This is even more powerful when negotiating a sale and a customer asks for a discount; "I can give you a 3.75% discount for paying cash because I won't have to pay credit card processing fees." Always let them know why and how you are giving an accurate discount; it preserves the value and integrity of the product or service.

11. Fewer Choices

Limit the number of options you give to your audience. Too many choices shut the brain down. How many of you have gone into a restaurant with a menu so big, with so many options that you feel overwhelmed and don't know what to choose to eat? If you are a Realtor, do not show 20 houses; do your homework and show only three to five houses. If you sell clothing, offer the sweater in red, white, or black; not red, white, black, purple, yellow, or green. In training, offer one or two follow-up options, not eight. The more options presented will add confusion to the decision-making process and will lead to nothing being accomplished.

12. Ask Permission

Asking permission makes others feel like they are in charge. It gives them perceived power and you have a better chance of their compliance. You can ask them questions like: "Can I share with you my suggestions?" "Is it OK to tell you what I would recommend?" "Can I tell you what I would do?" It is perfectly fine to ask generic questions like this while you are speaking in front of a group. It makes the entire audience feel like they are active participants in your presentation.

13. Be Memorable

Give your audience a positive memorable experience. Being creative with your content and incorporating a couple wild and amazing touches will make your presentation stand-out. This will change depending on the content of your presentation and who your audience is. Be fun, creative and think *outside of the box*.

14. Think Emotionally

People don't think logically, they think emotionally. People don't like to be sold, but they like to buy. People don't like being forced into a decision but enjoy free will in making their own choices. Use your language skills and body language techniques learned in these chapters to let people think that the choices they made were of their own free-will.

15. Fair and Honest

"Can I ask you a fair and honest question?" Asking people this question implies subconsciously that you are a fair and honest person. This perception of honesty will permeate all aspects of your program.

16. Simplicity

People are lazy and want simplicity in their lives. The more you can stress how your training, product, or service will simplify their professional or personal life, the quicker they will comply with your request. Your training program needs to solve the audience's obstacles in advance, even before they know they have a pending obstacle.

17. No Questions

When working with an audience, never give them the opportunity to disrupt you by asking questions. Questions cause disasters! There is always one person in an audience who thinks they know more than you. Allowing questions steals your energy and diminishes your perception of expertise. You can preface your presentation like this, "Before we begin, you must respect the fact that I have 2 hours of content to cover in 50 minutes. Therefore, we do not have time for questions or interruptions. If you think of a question, just write it down and send me an email or ask me in the hallway after I'm done."

18. Humor

Humor builds bonds and lowers resistance. Please remember only humor, no jokes! Most people cannot properly tell jokes, so you need to find the funny in previous situations which pertain to the content of your presentation. A humorous relatable story will make you and your content life-like! Never make fun of someone in your audience, always keep the humor based on a neutral topic. NO political or religious humor! Self-deprecating humor about yourself is fine.

19. Too Expensive

If a client or prospect tells you that your proposal is *too expensive*, your comeback is, "Compared to what?" That comeback makes them explain the justification to their statement and gives you a better idea on how, and to what, they are judging your proposal. Maybe you are offering more services than a competitor and if so, you could remove and adjust your proposal to be equally comparable.

20. Point Out Negatives

Point out any negative aspects of your proposal or training materials first before they do. This makes you appear more trustworthy and shows you are aware of any drawbacks. Being proactive in this manner deflates their ego and any boisterous negativity which could derail your program. "I know we are a few dollars higher than some competitors, but we include a 10 year warranty, while theirs is for only 4 years."

Chapter 15

Putting It All Together

Throughout this book, you have been given dozens of tips, tools, tricks, and techniques to either help you lay a foundation on your new journey of becoming a professional trainer or to take your existing training career to an elevated level. Albeit, you cannot use every item we have discussed in each of the training programs you develop; you have to be selective and use the best tips for the optimum effect on your audience. Those effects will vary based on the content of your presentation and the individuals in your audience. The lessons you have learned are not worthwhile unless you put them into action!

Do Something

As the powerful quote above reminds us...doing *something* is always better than doing *nothing*. Don't worry about waiting until your presentation is *just perfect* before you start presenting the contents. Start with what you have and improve on it at each upcoming teaching encounter. Think of it as a constantly improving and evolving product.

The software industry, especially Microsoft, taught us this valuable lesson. They release a new piece of software and offer frequent upgrades as they refined the original version. Your training programs are the same, you won't know what needs to be refined or changed until you start delivering the contents and receive feedback from your audience. Just start by doing something!

Price's Law

Are you familiar with the old saying, "If you want something done, give it to the busiest person?" Do you ever feel you are that *busy person*; always getting new projects assigned to your unending workload? Did you ever think there might be some scientific research supporting that old saying?

Back in 1963, Dr. Derek Price noticed a disparity in faculty journal articles and decided to do some research. He saw only a few people writing the majority of the research articles. His findings were coined as *Price's Law*:

Price's Law says 50% of work at a company is done by a small number of people. Specifically, it says: 50% of work is done by the square root of the number of employees.

So, let's look at the numbers: if a university published 100 journal articles and there are a total of 25 professors, then by applying Price's Law, we see that 5 professors wrote 50 articles, and the other 50 articles were written by the remaining 20 professors. This same formula can be extrapolated across any workplace environment, where the square root of the total employees does 50% of the work, while the remaining majority of employees slack-off on doing the other 50% of the work. So yes, there is scientific research proving that the busiest employees do the most amount of work!

Price's Law is a refined formulation of Lotka's Law describing the unequal distribution of productivity in most areas of creativity. Parallel to Price's Law is Zipf's Law which describes the unequal distribution of words in language usage; and the Pareto Principle, also known as the 80/20 rule in economics.

A Vast Future

Workplace training careers can be found in: nonprofit, government, healthcare, religion, insurance, hospitality, academia, large corporations, and small business. In many organizations, the trainer is the person who knows the most about the entire operation because they interact with all departments. You will become proficient in: new policies, new procedures, software implementations, product launches, governmental compliance laws, customer service, cultural competency, immigration, production cycles, and a host of other business processes. Your open-mindedness and ability to adapt to new situations, while seeing how the individual pieces fit together to run an entire operation, will make you an awesome trainer!

The training industry took a huge hit during the 2008 recession, but bounced back tremendously prior to the 2020 worldwide pandemic. A report published by ResearchandMarkets.com estimated in 2018 that the global workplace training market was valued at $368 billion USD. The industry's resilience is yet to be determined post 2020-

2021 global pandemic, but is expected to bounce back as it did post 2008. However, as we mentioned in a previous chapter, maybe some differences in operations, like more technology related learning modalities; with less large-group classroom settings.

Constant Improvement

Being a professional in any field means constant personal improvement; including your appearance and wardrobe to stay current with professional trends. More importantly though, is continual improvement in your knowledge base. You must stay abreast of all technological improvements as they relate not only to your particular industry, but also to teaching and training. This book has covered the latest research in a multitude of cross-platform fields in order to give you a solid well-rounded foundation. It will be up to you to stay current on the latest research in the fields of: public speaking, mind dynamics, body language, sales, persuasion, psychology, teaching methodologies, spatial proxemics, and communication skills. Also, it wouldn't hurt if you took a couple workshops in acting, stand-up, and improv comedy; just to enhance your comfort level interacting with groups and hecklers.

The fact that you purchased this book and took the time to study the lessons contained within these pages proves you are one of Price's square root few! I have faith in you, and you should have a strong faith in yourself. You will have a positive impact on people's personal and professional lives with the content you teach. Go out and change the world!

Much success on your exciting career, Ken

Study Exam Questions

Chapter 1

1. What is your opinion on the speaker/trainer bias example?
2. What previous personal encounters have you had which impacted your views on this debate?

Chapter 2

1. A fool may _____, but a wise man _____.
2. _____ speaking is delivering detailed information, while _____ speaking is stirring emotions, and _____ speaking is asking for your audience to do something.
3. Is speaking considered an art or a science? Why?
4. List two temporary or permanent bioorganic or neuromuscular issues that could hinder your ability to speak properly.
5. Is speech considered stimulating or transferring process?
6. Out of the twelve characteristics and personality traits listed, which ones do you have mastered, and which ones will you need to work on to become a better effective speaker?
7. Training + Ability + _____ = Success.

Chapter 3

1. The mind resides within the physical brain and is considered to be comprised of two parts, the _____ and the _____.

2. Found in the brain stem, this component is important for filtering sensory information.
3. _____ is the first requisite for effective speaking.
4. Why is a listener's attention important if you are speaking?
5. What are the Eight Axioms of Association and why are they crucial to developing training programs?
6. What are the two types of imagination?
7. What is the most powerful trigger to activate within your audience?
8. How could you use one of the five theories of emotion to stimulate your audience?
9. Give us an example of how you have used the process of reasoning in your life.

Chapter 4

1. What are the four components of the vocal mechanism?
2. Explain pitch, intensity, and quality.
3. How would a vocal coach help you in your speaking career?
4. Words are made up of _____ and _____.
5. Good word pronunciation comes from proper _____.
6. Your _____ is most reflected in your speech.

Chapter 5

1. _____ speaks louder than words.
2. An audience can really tell a beginning trainer by their _____.

3. What percentage of information we receive is non-verbally?
4. What you do is _____ times more informative than what you say.

Chapter 6
1. Where does your intuition live?
2. Our three-fold consciousness is equated to _____ hierarchy of needs.
3. Creativity and imagination is in the _____, while logic is found in the _____ brain.
4. Define proxemics.
5. If someone is standing 18 inches to 48 inches from you, they are considered to be in your _____ space.
6. Why should you never raise your hand or arms above your shoulders in a speaking situation?
7. What is your personal preference on the use of a podium?

Chapter 7
1. Who is considered the father of needs assessment work?
2. Why is a needs analysis process so important to a successful training program?
3. What is the difference between a need and a want?
4. Give an example of an open-ended question and closed-ended question.
5. Give an example of an extensive and intensive sampling group.
6. What does SWOT stand for?

Chapter 8

1. What is your opinion on the differences between children and adult learning theories?
2. What is the difference between andragogy and pedagogy?
3. Why is Bloom's Taxonomy important in workplace training?
4. What are the three learning styles?
5. How would you incorporate at least one of Gardner's Multiple Intelligences into a training program?
6. What makes the Montessori Method of schooling so different? Do you think it is more effective than traditional teaching methods?
7. How have generational issues impacted you in a workplace setting?
8. Describe a barrier to learning which you have witnessed in the past.
9. How will you make sure that you are a captivating trainer?

Chapter 9

1. Describe ADDIE.
2. As a student, do you prefer instructor-led or self-paced training and why?
3. Have you previously witnessed difficult behaviors in a learning environment? How was it handled?

Chapter 10

1. Where do you see the best application for the Socratic Method in workplace training?
2. What are a couple Socratic questions you could develop for your workplace?

Chapter 11

3. Why is assessment so important to the training process?
4. In the USA, you should speak and teach to your audience as if they were _____ graders.
5. A self-motivated student will use this type of assessment to gauge themselves.
6. What is one thing you cannot teach but seems to be lacking in society, today?

Chapter 12

1. What is your favorite ice breaker in this section?
2. Design your own personal ice breaker for use in your training sessions.

Chapter 13

1. Are there any other questions you would add to this list?

Chapter 14

1. Out of these 20 persuasion action tips, what three would you implement immediately into your professional life? And how?

Chapter 15

1. _____ is better than perfect!
2. Describe Price's Law.

Study Exam Answers

Chapter 1
1. Essay
2. Essay

Chapter 2
1. Talk, speaks
2. Exposition, argument, appeal
3. Both
4. Head cold, allergies, stutter, stroke related slurred speech, smoker's voice.
5. Stimulating
6. Essay
7. Will power

Chapter 3
1. Conscious, subconscious
2. RAS-Reticular Activation System
3. Clear thinking
4. Essay
5. Essay, + contiguity, similarity, contrast, cause and effect, frequency, vividness, recency, primacy.
6. Productive, reproductive
7. Emotion
8. Essay
9. Essay

Chapter 4
1. Motor, vibrator, resonator, articulator
2. Essay

3. Essay
4. Vowels, consonants
5. Enunciation
6. Education level or cultural development

Chapter 5
1. Body language
2. Stage freight or nervousness
3. 93%
4. 13

Chapter 6
1. Subconscious
2. Maslow's
3. Right, left
4. Essay ["the study of human space and the effects that population density has on behavior, communication, and social interaction."]
5. Personal
6. Essay [Triggers childhood memories or abuse.]
7. Essay

Chapter 7
1. Professor Roger Kaufman
2. Essay
3. Essay
4. Essay
5. Essay
6. Strengths, weaknesses, opportunities, threats

Chapter 8
1. Essay
2. Essay
3. Essay

4. Visual, auditory, kinesthetic or see, hear, feel
5. Essay
6. Essay
7. Essay
8. Essay
9. Essay

Chapter 9
1. Essay
2. Essay
3. Essay

Chapter 10
1. Essay
2. Essay

Chapter 11
3. Essay
4. 8th
5. Ipsative Assessment
6. Common sense or street smarts

Chapter 12
1. Essay
2. Essay

Chapter 13
1. Essay

Chapter 14
1. Essay

Chapter 15
1. Done
2. Essay

Bibliography & References

Bloom, Benjamin. *Taxonomy of Educational Objectives, Handbook 1: Cognitive Domain.* Boston: Addison-Wesley Longman Ltd., 1956.

Bramson, Robert. *Coping With Difficult People.* New York: Dell Books, 1981

Branch, Robert Maribe. *Instructional Design: The ADDIE Approach.* New York: Springer, 2014.

Bruce, Anne. *Speak For A Living: An Insider's Guide To Building A Speaking Career.* Alexandria, VA: ASTD Press, 2008.

Carnegie, Dale. *How To Win Friends And Influence People.* 1936. Reprint. New York: Pocket Books, 1990.

Chasen, Jim and Hodges, Lynn. *Teach With Style: Creative Tactics For Adult Learning.* Alexandria, VA: ASTD Press, 2012.

Gardner, Howard. *Frames of Mind: Theory of Multiple Intelligences.* New York: Basic Books, 1983.

Gardner, Howard. *Multiple Intelligences: New Horizons.* New York: Basic Books, 2006.

Giblin, Les. *How To Have Confidence and Power In Dealing With People.* New York: Prentice Hall, 1985.

Hall, Edward T. *The Silent Language.* New York: Anchor Books, 1973.

Hansen, Mark Victor and Batten, Joe. *The Master Motivator.* New York: Barnes and Noble, 1995.

Hogan, Kevin. *The Psychology of Persuasion: How To Persuade Others To Your Way Of Thinking.* Gretna, LA: Pelican Publishing, 1996.

Hogan, Kevin. *The Science Of Influence: How To Get Anyone To Say Yes In 8 Minutes Or Less.* Hoboken, NJ: John Wiley and Sons, 2005.

Kaufman, Roger and Guerra-Lopez, Ingrid. *Needs Assessment For Organizational Success.* Alexandria, VA: Association for Talent Development, 2013.

King, Larry. *How To Talk To Anyone, Anytime, Anywhere: The Secrets Of Good Communication.* New York: Crown, 1995.

Knowles, Dr. Eric and Linn, Jay. *Resistance And Persuasion.* Hove, UK: Psychology Press, 2003.

Knowles, Dr. Malcolm. *The Modern Practice of Adult Education: Andragogy Versus Pedagogy.* Cambridge, UK: Cambridge Book Co., 1988.

Lakhani, Dave. *Persuasion: The Art Of Getting What You Want.* Hoboken, NJ: John Wiley and Sons, 2005.

Mandino, Og. *The Greatest Salesman In The World.* New York: Bantam Books, 1983.

Marzano, Robert and Kendall, John. The New Taxonomy Of Educational Objectives. Thousand Oaks, CA: Corwin, 2006.

McCarthy, Bernice and McCarthy, Dennis. *Teaching Around The 4MAT Cycle: Designing Instruction For Diverse Learners With Diverse Learning Styles*. Thousand Oaks, CA: Corwin, 1978.

Mehrabian, Albert. *Nonverbal Communication*. Oxford, UK: Routledge, 2007.

Montessori, Maria. *The Montessori Method*. South Carolina: CreateSpace, 2014.

National Speakers Association. *Paid To Speak: Best Practices For Building A Successful Speaking Business*. Austin, TX: Greenleaf, 2011.

Plutchik, Robert and Kellerman, Henry. *Theories of Emotion: Volume 1*. New York: Academic Press, 1980.

Qubein, Nido. *Communicate Like A Pro*. Hoboken, NJ: Prentice-Hall, 1983.

Reiman, Tonya. *The Power Of Body Language: How To Succeed In Every Business And Social Encounter*. New York: Gallery Books, 2008.

Ruiz, Don Miguel. *The Four Agreements: A Practical Guide To Personal Freedom A Toltec Wisdom Book.* San Rafael, CA: Amber-Allen Publishing, 1997.

Teeters, Jim and Hodges, Lynn. *Teach With Style: Creative Tactics For Adult Learning*. Alexandria, VA: ASTD Press, 2013.

Waitley, Denis. *Seeds Of Greatness: 10 Best Kept Secrets Of Total Success*. Grand Rapids, MI: Fleming H Revell Co., 1983.

Walsby, Harold. *The Domain of Ideologies: A Study Of The Origin, Development, And Structure Of Ideologies*. UK: Social Science Association, 1946.

www.brainyquote.com

www.dictionary.com

www.novoed.com

www.skepticwiki.org

www.taigoodwin.com

www.wikipedia.com

Research References

Chapter 8

Frontiers. Learning styles: *A once hot debate redshifts*.
ScienceDaily. ScienceDaily, 11 May 2017.
www.sciencedaily.com/releases/2017/05/170511095045.htm

University of Arizona. *Learning is optimized when we fail 15% of
the time*. ScienceDaily. ScienceDaily, 5 November 2019.
www.sciencedaily.com/releases/2019/11/191105113457.htm

Chapter 9

University of Nottingham. *Virtual reality training could improve
employee safety*. ScienceDaily. ScienceDaily, 16 September
2019.
www.sciencedaily.com/releases/2019/09/190916212516.htm

University of Maryland. People recall information better through
virtual reality. ScienceDaily. ScienceDaily, 13 June 2018.
www.sciencedaily.com/releases/2018/06/180613162613.htm

University of Colorado Denver. *Video games can be highly
effective training tools, study shows: Employees learn more,
forget less, master more skills*. ScienceDaily. ScienceDaily, 20
October 2010.
www.sciencedaily.com/releases/2010/10/101019171854.htm

Chapter 11

Association for Psychological Science. *Science of training and
development in organizations: What really matters, what really*

works. ScienceDaily. ScienceDaily, 13 June 2012.
www.sciencedaily.com/releases/2012/06/120613133148.htm

Chapter 14

National Institute for Physiological Sciences (2012, November 9). *Scientific explanation to why people perform better after receiving a compliment*. ScienceDaily. ScienceDaily, 19 November 2012.
www.sciencedaily.com/releases/2012/11/121109111517.htm

Additional References

VARK: www.vark-learn.com

Leitner System (Spaced-Repetition):

    www.mometrix.com

    www.mindedge.com

4MAT: www.4mat4learning.com.au

Socratic Method:

    www.criticalthinking.org

    www.trigonweb.com

Additional Useful References:

    www.cdc.goc_healthyschools

    www.centerforbodylanguage.com

    www.feather.ca

    www.frontiers.org

    www.lincs.ed.gov

    www.publicspeakking.com

    www.td.org

    www.trainingmag.com

Index

About Ken Owens

Ken Owens is a human-potential consultant in the areas of motivation, training, and personal development. He has 30+ years of corporate, nonprofit, government, and small business management experience; as well as being a former annual corporate $1 million sales producer.

Ken is a Certified Stress Management Consultant with International Association of Counselors and Therapists, Board Certified Hypnotherapist with American Board of Hypnotherapy and Professional Board of Hypnotherapy in Canada, Ordained Minister, Certified Sales Trainer, and a Certified Life Coach; and a former CEU granting trainer with: Nevada State Health Department, Nevada State Boards of Nursing and Pharmacy, and The Nevada Registry.

Ken blends his corporate sales experience with his training and counseling expertise; along with degrees in: Liberal Arts, Business Management, Mind Dynamics, Ethics, and Counseling/Therapy. Ken was the leading requested speaker while on the Speaker's Bureau at Wayne State University. He has spoken and conducted training programs in 47 of the 50 United States; along with Canada, Puerto Rico, The Bahamas, England, and Slovenia.

Ken is the international selling author of the book *Branding Your Character*. You have seen him on *ABC's Good Morning America,* and he is available to work with your organization.

TheKenOwens.com and **BrandingYourCharacter.com**

Ordering Information

For individual worldwide copies of this book:

Amazon.com
(Or the Amazon website specific to your country)

Case-lot orders for resale, educational, and non-profit purposes, contact your local book wholesaler through Ingram or Baker & Taylor. You may also inquire at:

PersonalDynamicsPublishing.com

For speaking/training opportunities from Ken:

TheKenOwens.com

Made in the USA
Columbia, SC
17 June 2024

36885405R00122